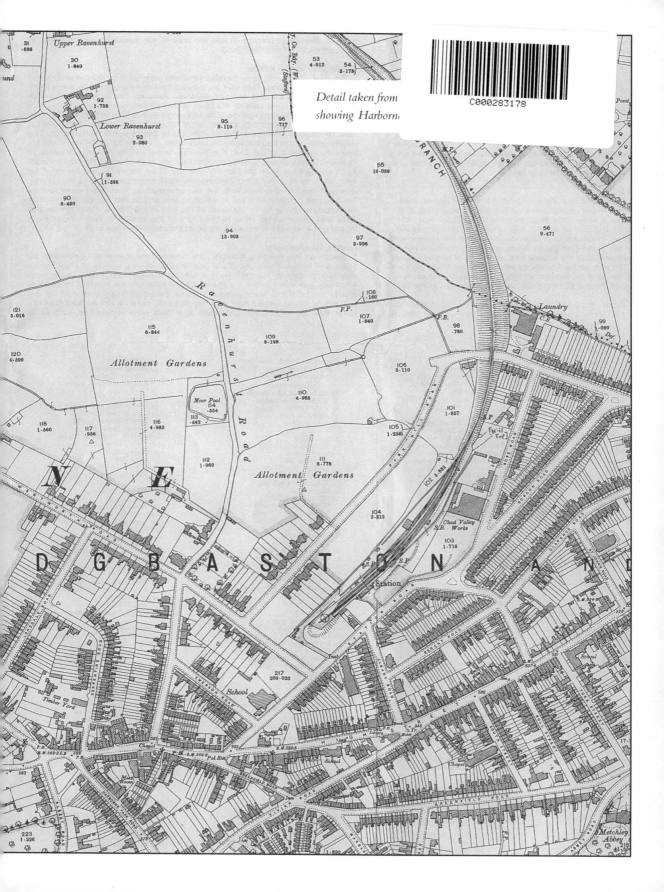

HARBORNE
A History

A tranquil scene in Harborne Park Road in 1960, photographed for the Harborne Society.

Harborne
A History

Edward Chitham

Phillimore

2004

Published by
PHILLIMORE & CO. LTD,
Shopwyke Manor Barn, Chichester, West Sussex, England

ISBN 1 86077 294 3

Printed and bound in Great Britain by
CAMBRIDGE PRINTING

Contents

List of Illustrations

Acknowledgements

The illustrations are largely taken from four collections: that of the Harborne Society, by permission of Mary Abbott and Phil Stokes; the Donald Wright collection at Harborne library, by permission of Wendy Carter and Mary Worrall; St Peter's church collection, by permission of Rev. Jo Evans; and the author's own collection. Many of the Harborne Society photographs reproduced were taken by Maurice Evans, while the St Peter's collection was preserved by Brenda Durbin. Additional illustrations are by permission of Lichfield Record Office. Other drawings and maps are based on various sources given below.

Harborne Society collection: 17, 29, 30, 43, 58, 59, 60, 61, 62, 67, 68, 69, 70, 71, 78, 80, 81, 82, 83, 85, 86, 87, 93, 100, 102, 106, 108, 109, 111, 116, 122, 128, 129, 133, 135, 136.

Harborne Library collection (mainly collected by Donald Wright): 14, 15, 16, 32, 33, 34, 40, 45, 51, 52, 63, 64, 73, 84, 90, 91, 92, 94, 95, 96, 114, 118, 119, 120, 121, 153.

St Peter's collection: 19, 49, 72, 88, 105, 112, 124, 126, 127, 130, 131, 134, 137, 138, 139, 140, 144, 147, 148, 149, 150, 151, 152.

Author's collection: 1, 2, 3, 4, 5, 6, 7, 8, 9, 10, 11, 12, 13, 18, 20, 21, 22, 23, 24, 27, 28, 31, 35, 36, 37, 38, 39, 41, 42, 43, 44, 46, 47, 48, 50, 53, 54, 55, 57, 65, 66, 74, 75, 76, 77, 79, 89, 97, 98, 99, 103, 104, 107, 110, 113, 114, 115, 117, 123, 125, 132, 141, 142, 143, 145, 146, 154, 155 and frontispiece.

Lichfield Record Office: 25, 26 (wills collection), 56 (tithe plan from Birch/Hinckley collection).

Rachel Chitham-Mosley: 101, 156.

Research for the historical narrative has been helped by librarians and archivists at Staffordshire Record Office, Stafford; Lichfield Record Office; Birmingham Archives; Birmingham Library Local History Department; Birmingham Museum and Art Gallery; Smethwick Library and Harborne Library. Extra photographs were taken by John Chitham.

Special thanks for access to their collections are due to Jo Curtis, Younis Zaman, Wendy Carter, Mary Worrall and their predecessors. My research on Harborne history began with advice from 'Billy' Hardwick and continued with help from Donald Wright as well as Rev. Michael Counsell, Dr Robert Hetherington and many others. A very great help during recent Harborne research was provided by the transcripts of the Harborne tithe apportionment and register by A.C. and D. Guest of Smethwick, to whom I am most grateful for their gift of a copy of the apportionment. Secondary sources used include Donald Wright's *An Account of Harborne* and *The Victoria County History of Warwickshire*, Vol. VII.

ONE

Boundaries and Beginnings

The old rhyme says, 'Hungry Harborne, proud and poor; a washerwoman stands at every door'. So what made Harborne so hungry, and why were there so many washerwomen in the 19th century, when this rhyme originated? Harborne stands on a high peninsula, and in prehistoric times was covered with forest. There is little trace of earlier peoples in this part of the Midlands, other than the 'burnt mounds' along the course of the Bourn brook. The purpose of these mounds of burnt stones is very uncertain, but they are evidence that pre-Roman people traced the course of the brook as it wound along the valley which would later divide Harborne from Northfield parish.

Today much of Harborne is densely populated, a Birmingham suburb where house prices are high and roads narrow. Long queues of traffic form down the High Street and up the hills which feed it: War Lane, Harborne Park Road, Lordswood Road. What intriguing names these roads have! Further west we can see what Harborne was once like: two parks, two golf courses, and an open landscape culminating in Woodgate City Farm preserve the outlines of old fields, with field paths and lanes reminding us of the terrain which existed until the middle of the 20th century. Or we can walk the valleys of the two main brooks, which run in the same courses as they did in Anglo-Saxon times, forming the boundaries of Harborne. These brooks, the Bourn and the Chad, with the Moor Pool, provided the resources for the 19th-century washerwomen. Like these women, Harborne residents over the years have made the community. The area boasts few men and women of fame, but there have been many 'ordinary' characters.

Surprisingly, boundaries do not always change over time. For many years the City of Birmingham has placed boundary signs in Harborne, two to the north, two south and one west. The southern marks and one of the northern ones probably coincide with Domesday boundaries, and the southern boundary is particularly significant.

Signs at Harborne Mill and near the bottom of Stonehouse Hill mark the boundary brook, the 'bourne' (Scots 'burn') which makes up half of Harborne's name. This boundary has not only been a parish and manor boundary, but the county and diocesan boundary, and almost a national boundary in Anglo-Saxon times between the Saxon Hwicce and the Anglian Mercians. The 'Har' in Harborne is cognate with 'hoar' in 'hoar frost' and 'hoary headed'. It

I *Abbot Nicholas of Halesowen, 13th-century lord of the manor of Harborne and Smethwick.*

means *grey*, but because grey stones were often used as boundaries, the word came to mean *boundary*. So Harborne's name twice emphasises that the place is a boundary. (An earlier, Celtic, derivation given by Kenward in his 1885 book *Harborne and its Surroundings* has no factual basis.)

War Lane seems to have the same derivation, and means 'boundary lane'. The eastern boundary is marked by the Chad brook (St Chad was Bishop of Lichfield), running from Bearwood, under the Hagley Road, down to allotments at the foot of Harborne Hill. This area is still liable to flooding after heavy rain, and was previously very swampy. From Bearwood to Nursery Road the other side of the boundary is Edgbaston, Warwickshire. The swamp may historically have been thought of as no man's land, part of Harborne Heath, which extends across Nursery Road to approximately St John's Road. (A map of 1806 questions exactly where the boundary is at this point; perhaps not at the *Green Man*, but at Kingscote Road.) Harborne's boundary with Quinton

is more difficult. Much of Quinton was formerly 'the township of Ridgacre', part of Halesowen parish, taken into Shropshire in 1177 after the transfer of the manor and parish to the family of Owen, Prince of North Wales. But not all Quinton went into Shropshire; near the modern West Boulevard is a strip of land which remained as part of Warley 'Wigorn' (i.e. Worcestershire). The Harborne/Quinton boundary at this point ran dead straight across the middle of fields. However, the land on both sides was owned by Tennal Hall. It looks as though the Warley Wigorn strip may once have been in Harborne, and that Halesowen (Ridgacre) boundary may have been roughly where the present White Road is. Another possibility is that all Tennal Hall lands were once in Halesowen, leaving the *Court Oak* (once perhaps an ancient tree, now marked by the public house) as the original boundary mark.

The major change in Harborne's boundaries is on the north, where the Hagley Road now separates Harborne from Smethwick, the City of Birmingham and the Metropolitan Borough of Sandwell (and, some say, 'Birmingham' and 'The Black Country'). This division appears in Domesday, where 'Horeborne' has one 'carucate' of land, held by one Robert, and 'Smedewic' two carucates, which a certain William held together with five carucates in Tipton. Both these manors were parts of the Lichfield manor of the Bishop of Chester (the same diocese as Lichfield, under a different name). Soon, however, Harborne and Smethwick manors congealed, coming in line with the ecclesiastical parish. Thus it remained until 1709, and in fact until late in the 19th century it is often hard to identify houses, land and people in Smethwick; the old documents simply record them as 'Parish of Harborne'. This concept of a single parish of Harborne, stretching from Harborne Mill to West Bromwich Albion football ground, outlasted tentative divisions in the 1730s and 1840s.

The Romans must have had a road through Harborne, leading from Metchley Camp to Greensforge beyond Kingswinford, but it is quite untraceable. Metchley itself has been investigated by archaeologists on a number of occasions, but it lies outside the scope of this book. An alleged Roman well was discovered near the Field House in Harborne Park Road in the 19th century but proof that it was Roman is lacking.

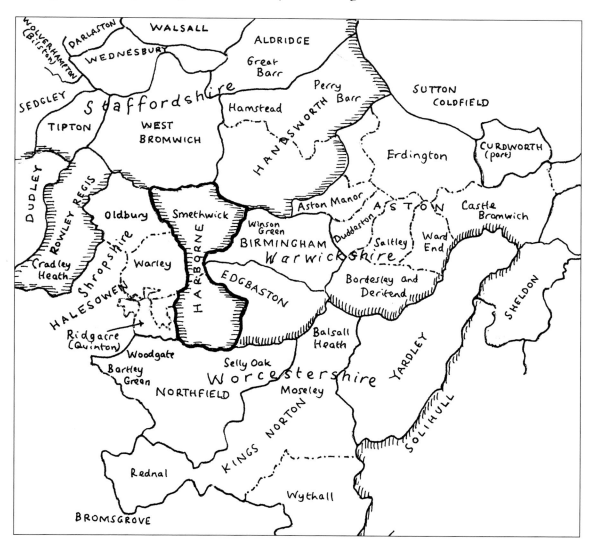

2 Location map of traditional Harborne parish, with its neighbours in Staffordshire, Warwickshire, Worcestershire and Shropshire.

3 *The residual hollow in Lightwoods Park near Galton Road which marks the boundary between the old Harborne parish and Warley.*

Even Anglo-Saxon origins are hard to discern. It is possible that the boundary between Harborne (Lichfield) and North-field (Worcester) dates from the period after 672 when Worcester diocese was formed, but it may be older. The division between Warwickshire and Staffordshire followed, after the fortification of Stafford in 913.

However, eccclesiastical (parish and diocesan) boundaries do not always coincide with secular (manor and county) bounda-ries. The location of St Peter's church, on the central hill in Harborne, does suggest an early foundation, perhaps with some small huts round it. St Peter is a dedication sometimes given to churches placed on an old sacred rock, and this may be so here.

The church, overlooking the whole area, may well have been built in a defensive position; the tower walls are more than five feet thick. Perhaps the church tower was a watch tower as well, from which enemies could be spotted at a distance. This is only guesswork, and the supposed Anglo-Saxon cross base discovered under St Peter's church floor in the 1970s is more likely to have been the base of the door of an 18th-century renovation. It is now in the renewed vicarage garden. Though the Rev. Angus MacIntyre thought that a stone built into the south transept might have been Anglo-Saxon, there is no proof of this.

Still we are left with puzzles. We do not know the reason for the 'egg-timer' shape of the original Harborne parish, with its narrow neck at Bearwood. If it did once include Edgbaston, why was that parish left in Warwickshire? For much of its existence, Harborne 'manor' is seen as a part of the enormous 'Longdon' manor, which also included Tipton and many manors in mid-Staffordshire. Longdon was part of Offlow Hundred, and this obscure hill near Tamworth would have been a central meeting place for stewards or other representatives of the villages and hamlets of much of the southern half of the county. In Anglo-Saxon times, religious Harborne (as well as Edgbaston) became a 'peculiar' of the Dean and Chapter of Lichfield. This meant that Lichfield cathedral could control the priests at Harborne, and the influence was felt until the mid-19th century.

Harborne parish and manor, even including Smethwick, is much smaller than neighbouring Halesowen, which included Oldbury, Quinton, Romsley, Cradley, Frankley and Illey, or the large Aston parish which included Erdington, Ward End, Digbeth and Water Orton. This suggests that Harborne once took in other places, perhaps Handsworth and even possibly West Bromwich. This would make Harborne an original 'minster' church.

From the south, east and north-west Harborne is approached by climbing hills. Apart from the brooks mentioned, there are several others running in hollows, sometimes still visible though often culverted. Two of these meet on the municipal golf course near the 'Hilly Fields path'; the western one is called Welsh House brook, while the other, which has no name, runs down from Earls Court Road, where ancient willow trees mark an earlier pond, via Queen's Park (where there was also a pond) to Harts Green, where it is now culverted but can still be heard on days of torrential rain under Vicarage Road. It joins the visible brook at Tibbets Lane. Tributaries of the Chad brook ran on the site of Blakeney Avenue and across Lordswood School fields, the second of which can be seen at its confluence with the Chad. Despite all this water, the only viable place for a watermill in ancient times was at Harborne Mill on the Selly Oak boundary. Across the Hagley Road, on the other side of the watershed, the waters of the Shireland brook finally flow, like the rest, into the Trent, but via the Tame without joining the Rea until much later. There was no mill in this area, 'Thimblemill' in Bearwood being in Warley, part of Halesowen parish and not in Harborne.

TWO

Mapping Medieval Harborne

edieval feudal society produced communities based on land cultivation and fealty to the lord of the manor. Social institutions are similar in many communities, and the effects can be seen many years after they have passed away. There are no medieval maps of Harborne, but traces lingered on from which we can construct a likely medieval picture. There was certainly a hall, later one of the 'capital messuages'. This would be occupied by a steward, since the lord of the manor was actually at various times in Halesowen Abbey, Longdon or Lichfield. The hall was located where Harborne Hall is now, but its appearance would be very different, a one-storey thatched building of timber. Below this, extending down what is now Grove Lane, was the Park, originally a deer park, probably enclosed with a fence. Traces of this remain in later documents as 'Park Fields' and in the current name of Parkville Avenue. This hall had its 'fishpond', which still remains in the hall grounds. Nearby we can imagine the church, St Peter's, its tower renewed in the 14th or 15th century. The nave of this church lasted, with renovations and repairs, until 1827, and parts may still remain on the northern side. There was perhaps a house for a priest

on the site of the rectory farm, or possibly the current vicarage site. Apart from this, there must have been some peasant houses, impermanent and leaky, but we cannot tell where. This was no nucleated village, but a scattered parish with isolated farms among the woodland.

It is well known that medieval agriculture worked the 'three-field system', with strips tilled by each tenant in each field. Traces of such a system (with more than three small fields) remained in Harborne as late as the 18th century, and one can still see the faint outline of the strips on the cricket field. Around the scattered and rough huts that was medieval Harborne were the Green Field (as its name implies, near Greenfield Road); Inchmore (or Hinchmore or Winchmore) Field (between modern Vicarage Road and War Lane); Riddings/Weddings Field (the modern cricket and hockey pitches with land near Bishop's Croft), and the Leyfield, along what is now the southern end of Lordswood Road. Much of the rest was 'the Lord's waste': Harborne Heath and some of the western side. To the north, Lord's Wood extended from modern Elm Tree Road to the *King's Head*. Later generations asserted a common right here concerning firewood and timber. The Marquess of Anglesey, lord

4 *Harborne Cricket Club ground, showing residual signs of strip farming on the 'Wedding Field'.*

of Longdon Manor, was still claiming an interest in the wood in the 19th century, and presumably the name 'Lord's' indicates this claim. Beyond this, the name Bearwood may be taken literally. Bears once roamed where now the *Bear Tavern* stands. The hazardous journey to the Smethwick end of the parish, in which were a number of old isolated settlements, ran along a causeway through more forest. It seems, though, that beyond the King's Head Cross (earlier called The Crossways) there were more beeches than oaks.

The name 'Lightwood(s)' is very ancient in Harborne. It survives in Lightwoods Park, on the northern side of the Hagley Road and Lightwoods School, Warley. It was often used as an alternative name for Lord's Wood, which was sometimes known as Great Lightwood. Little Lightwood was its extension southwards, to what is now Elm Tree Road. South of this was Burnt Heath (the area now covered by Wood Lane and Woodville Road); perhaps this too had been woodland. Later on, village sports and races were held here. But the name Lightwood also occurs in two other places, on the east of Lordswood Road, where a piece of charity land is named 'Lightwood als [or] Gorsty Croft' in 1591, and in a field on the farm at Hill Top (Bedford), near what is now Rose Road police station, which was called Nagg's Wood in the 19th century but was previously 'Nagg Leightwood'. This is a mile away from the other field, but may indicate that much of the eastern side of the parish and manor was woodland, and that the name Lightwood was extensive over most of the

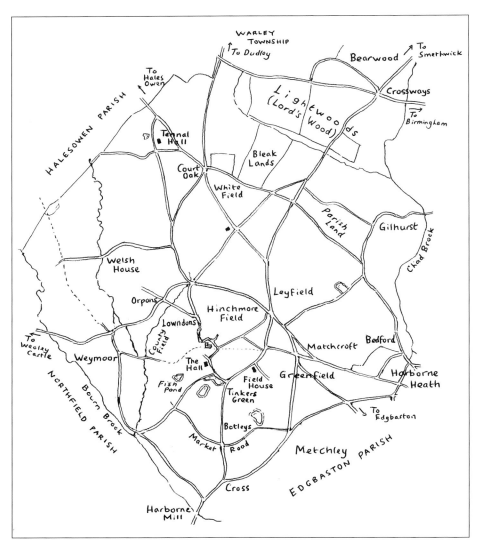

5 *Map showing the features of Harborne in the late Middle Ages.*

north and east of the district. Some scholars think its original meaning is 'hillside wood'. Another place-name implying a woodland origin is 'Stockings', a name for an area near Harts Green, and a third likely name is 'Riddings', so named after the peasants had rid themselves of trees at that point. Riddings Meadow was part of what is now Grove Park.

Apart from the scattering of dwellings near the church, there were a number of remote freeholdings; one may be the site of the later Manor House, Harrison's or Birches Green, near the top of the present Fellows Lane.

It is interesting that two small fields have the name 'Court Oak' at an early stage. This may indicate a place where the manor court was held, an oak being a familiar landmark in the cleared land. Another property later called a 'capital messuage' is Tennal Hall, and another Home Farm. Over the southern boundary lay the fortified manor house at Weoley Castle, enclosed and crenellated in 1264 by Roger de Somery, a member of the Dudley family. While he was building his new castle walls, a legal wrangle between Lichfield and Halesowen Abbey dragged on; it concerned control over Harborne church: who would have the right to nominate the priest, the abbot or the bishop? In 1270 a final decision handed the 'advowson' to Lichfield where it remained for six hundred years. Perhaps Roger's decision to fortify Weoley had some connection with the power struggle over the church.

Another landmark was the deep valley called Gilhurst, the configuration of which can still be seen in the nature walk off Gillhurst Road. This has now returned to its original wooded state. One of the documents referring to this dispute mentions Harborne church 'cum capellis'. The implication is that Harborne had more than one chapel depending on it. We know that one was Edgbaston, but any others are still to seek. Certainly there does not seem to be any trace within Harborne itself, and there is no record of an old chapel at Smethwick before the erection of the present 'old church' in 1732.

Communications in the Middle Ages were rough and dangerous. Wherever the Roman road ran, it had decayed by then and was no longer in use. A trace may possibly run along the course of Margaret Road, the edge of the Green Field. Links with Lichfield must have been needed, and we can reasonably assume a route following Lordswood Road; to the south this led past Harborne Mill towards Kings Norton, Bromsgrove and Worcester. This would also form the 'corpse road' where coffins would be carried in procession from Smethwick,

down through the oak woods to what is now Fellows Lane. An east to west road must have existed, but it was probably not the present Hagley Road. Another certain link would have been the lane from Weoley Castle towards Dudley, via Northfield Road, Tennal Road and Balden Road. The Middle Ages needed a supply of salt, and locally this was obtained from Droitwich. Its carriage would have required a passable road, perhaps Northfield Road through Shenley Fields.

By far the greatest local power was that of the lords of Weoley Castle. This great building, now a ruin, is situated just on the other side of Stonehouse brook, and so beyond Harborne's traditional boundaries. It is thought that the name derives from Saxon 'Weoh-Leah' meaning a wood or clearing in which there is a pagan temple. The site has been excavated on a number of occasions, and is considered to be the premier archaeological site in Birmingham. There seem to have been three periods of building, one from about 1100 to 1200, in which a timber-framed building was erected, with possibly a stone chapel; a second period from 1200 to 1260, when a stone hall was built, with two more wooden buildings including a farm; and a third period, when Roger de Somery fortified the whole castle. A description of the castle, made in 1424, says that the main entrance was in the north-west corner, and was reached by a drawbridge after passing the gatehouse. On the north was the guest wing and a chapel. The great hall was part of the eastern range, while opposite it were the bakehouse, brewhouse and stables. Archaeologists found evidence of the inhabitants' diet: beef, mutton, pork, venison, swan, heron, chicken, pike and hedgehog. Many of these creatures must

6 *Drawing of Weoley Castle in the late Middle Ages. The castle is several hundred metres outside Harborne, in Northfield parish.*

have been caught locally, along the valley of the Bourn brook and the fish in the specially created fishponds.

Weoley Castle fell into disrepair, and a farmhouse was built from the remains. Stone from the castle was used to build Stonehouse Farm, and even in the 19th century tenders for 'Weoley castle stone' were obtained in order to build Rowley Regis church. The yeoman farmers of the 18th century, such as William Green, attended Harborne parish church and had their own private pew there. The present Hilly Fields path owes its continuing existence to the importance of communications between Harborne old village and Weoley Castle.

Further away but even more influential was Halesowen Abbey. Its parish stretched to what is now West Boulevard through the area then known as Ridgacre, but land owned by Halesowen in Harborne was outside Halesowen parish. During the Black

Death of 1349, 81 of 203 males living in the wider Halesowen parish died. It is interesting that the lowest percentage of deaths was in Ridgacre, and this may suggest that the same would be true of Harborne. This could be due to the higher land in Ridgacre and Harborne, while Halesowen itself lies in the valley. One of Halesowen's five granges, or monastic storehouses, was on the Harborne border at Redhall, the name perhaps deriving from a Red Well in the area. In the 19th century Reddall Farm was just on the Quinton side of the boundary, but another small farm on the Harborne side was called both Redhall and Redhill. By 1535, when the lesser monasteries were on the point of dissolution, rent from land in Harborne was contributing £5 16s. to the abbey, and rent from Smethwick just over £16. Some of this rent may have come from 'St Mary Moor', land bordering the Bourn brook near the present Weymoor.

In the 14th century there was a form of taxation known as 'subsidy'. In 1327 eighteen substantial inhabitants of Harborne and Smethwick paid the tax. They were Adam de Whatecroft (Wheatcroft), Madoke Wyr, Will'o Doggyng, Joh'e de Clodeshale, Rob'to de Breuera, Will'o le spinnere, Henr' de Weleye, Will'mo de Birches, Joh'e Gregory, Will'o Burel, Will'mo de Oumbresley, Rad'o Attegorstes, Will'o filio Hugonis, Joh'o de Hasterleye, Rob'oatte lee and Joh'e le freemon. In this list we see for the first time a number of surnames developing which will be significant in Harborne history: Weoley, Birch, Hughes, Lea and Freeman. Altogether they contributed 39s. and 5d. to the Scottish war of King Edward III. Will'o Doggyng is called Bogging in the next subsidy list; a place-name 'Buggins' appears in a 17th-century will, and this was most probably where William lived. 'Spinners' is the name of a field near the bottom of Lordswood Road, and this may have been the holding of Will'o le spinnere.

This next subsidy roll was made in 1333, and some of the above still feature in it. Others have clearly died during the interval, and their places are taken by Thom' Fychet, John'e le Clerke, Henr' in le Lone, Rad'o Gorstus, Henr' atte Ruddynge and others. We can recognise here that our present system of surnames is developing, and that a number of these names may reflect places in Harborne, e.g. 'le Lee' (the lea), 'le Lone' (the lane), 'de Birches' (the birch trees). In general, there is no way that these locations can be recognised, but a later 'Wheatcroft' appears to be near *The Old House at Home*. Perhaps John'e le Clerke (John the Clerk or John Clark) had received his training in writing at Halesowen Abbey.

By 1429 a system of guardians of the peace had been established for Staffordshire. For Harborne, the two chosen were John Whatecroft (doubtless a descendant of Adam in the subsidy list) and Nicolas Thyknes. Both are labelled 'gentlemen' and both are required to take an oath against harbouring peace-breakers. 'Peace-breaking' was certainly common. In 1482, for example, a John Warley sued Humfrey Bandyke for breaking into his close at 'Horburn' and cutting down his trees and underwood. The tables were turned in 1484 when the same John (now spelt Wirley) was sued by

7 *The medieval tower of Harborne parish church (St Peter's). Most of the work is thought to be 14th-century, with the large window over the door from the 15th century.*

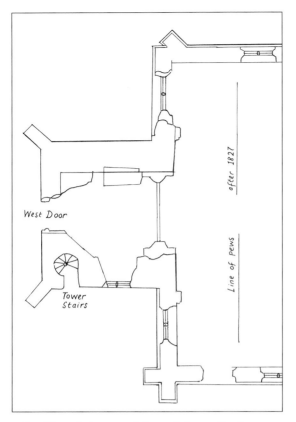

West Door

Tower Stairs

after 1827

Line of pews

8 *Plan of the ground floor of the medieval tower of Harborne church. This is from Yeoville Thomason's drawing in 1866. (Yeoville Thomason's 1866 plans, then at St Peter's)*

William Barkeley for breaking into his close and taking 'a stag worth 40 shillings'. John flouted the authority of the sheriff, who was ordered to arrest him and bring him before the court on the Octave of Holy Trinity.

It is hard to know what these legal cases actually signify. Legal fictions were sometimes used to effect land transfer. In 1519 we have an apparent dispute between 'William Wyllington' and 'George Byrch, deforciant' over two messuages (houses), 60 acres of land, 20 acres of meadow, 100 acres of pasture, 100 acres of wood, 10 acres of moor, 20 acres of furze and heath, and 10s. rent in 'Smethwyke in the parish of Harborne'. This is interesting in proving that George Birch, whose name recurs many times in Harborne history in the shape of different individuals, was already established in the parish and owned land in Smethwick. Later members of the family lived at Holt Hill near Roebuck Lane, as well as a number of farms in Harborne proper. Wyllington paid £60 for the eventual grant of land.

In the early to mid-16th century there were great ecclesiastical changes in England. The dissolution of Halesowen Abbey led to Harborne passing into crown hands. A register of all births, marriages and deaths had to be kept after 1538 in all parishes, and Harborne is lucky in having entries from 21 February of that year. The first entry records the burial of 'Henri Carles', whose family plays an important part in Harborne history and is remembered in Carless Avenue. A few years later an inventory of all church goods had to be made. Harborne then possessed a silver chalice, six altar crosses and two candlesticks, three bells in the 'stepull' (tower) and some vestments, 'one of velvet, one of damask', as well as copes, towels, handbells and other items. The churchwardens were John Baker and Richard Pedoke (Piddock). This suggests that the custom already existed of having one churchwarden for the Harborne side and one for Smethwick, as Baker was a name common in Harborne while the Piddocks lived in Smethwick.

THREE

Henry VIII to Queen Anne

Though it was King Henry VIII's doing, the confiscation of the manor of Harborne and its presentation to the Paget family is dated 1553, the first year of the reign of Queen Mary. This record seeems to reflect the fact that Harborne was still seen as part of the great Longdon manor. Until the 19th century Harborne had to send representatives to the Court Baron of Longdon, and manorial rights would be reasserted by the Anglesey family as late as the 1830s. However, there must have been some confusion over the manor, because the Warwickshire historian Dugdale is reported to have said that it belonged to the Dudleys. What is certain is that in 1554 Queen Mary 'restored' Harborne, with lands in Northfield, Sedgley and Dudley, to the Lords of Dudley Castle. In church affairs the parish of Harborne (including Smethwick) lay in the hands of the Dean and Chapter of Lichfield, forming part of an entity known as the Lichfield 'peculiar'. This link remained until the formation of Birmingham diocese in the early 20th century.

A persistent legend maintains that Queen Elizabeth passed through Harborne, staying at Tennal Hall on her way to Dudley. If this is so, the date would have been 27 July 1575, when the Queen visited Dudley Castle after being entertained at Kenilworth. There is nothing unlikely about the story, and indeed the Queen would have had to pass close by whatever route she took. The present Hagley Road was not at that time a favoured route. A highway entered Harborne Heath after crossing the swampy Chad brook at what is now Kingscote Road, and proceeded near Moor Pool, crossing the lane from Harborne to Gilhurst (Ravenhurst Road) and running along the back of what is now Oakham Road to meet Lordswood Road, then along Elm Tree Road towards the Court Oak, where the back lane is part of this once important route. If she travelled that way, the Queen would then be near Tennal Hall.

Tennal Hall was one of the most important houses in Harborne. Modified and rebuilt many times, it was divided into two in the 17th century. By 1593 it was occupied by the Milward family, who also had branches at Welsh House and Weymoor. The family were yeomen, minor gentry, but in no sense aristocrats. They could perhaps have put on a good feast for the Queen, but there is no proof. On the other hand, some resting place for her must have been found between Kenilworth and Dudley, and the Dudleys owned Harborne. Tennal Hall

9 *The remaining buildings at Harborne Mill. This was first a corn mill, then a blade mill, and the premises are now used by a number of small independent firms.*

was eventually plastered, so that the 'close studding' of the timbers was obscured, and this may have contributed to its demise in the 20th century.

In the 16th century and afterwards the vicar was an important figure. His salary was made up by selling the tithes payable on land in the 'glebe', i.e. the church land in the parish. In 1587 the tithe was leased to Thomas Chattock, who could then farm the tithes payable on corn. This provided a stipend of £12 for the vicar of the time, Raphael Norman. Chattock did, however, keep the right to live in the vicarage and had a small garden and orchard for himself. In time, the right to the tithes became a bone of contention, which was not settled until the 19th century. Later, Catherine Norman married Nicholas Pudsey, gentleman, the marriage taking place at Sutton Coldfield and their first child was appropriately christened Norman Pudsey. The Pudsey family then kept the tithes, passing them on to their heirs, despite moving to Seisdon beyond Wolverhampton. The vicar who followed Norman was Humphrey Fletcher. We can imagine sweet music wafting across the churchyard in the early 1600s, as Fletcher possessed a set of virginals. When he died in 1611 he left his cows, books and property to his wife, together with the tithes and the 'advowson' of the church.

Another prominent Midland family with a branch which lived in Harborne was the

Stanleys. In 1622 Roger Stanley was given the job of collecting rent for the Right Hon. Lord William Paget of Beaudesert (owner of the Longdon Manor). He must have occupied a position as steward, but, because the manor was also claimed by the Dudleys, it is hard to know exactly where he lived. Charles Stanley was in trouble in 1633 when he was alleged to have cut down trees on his land enough to make 3,000 faggots, without paying tithe. He then bound the faggots with cord, making 400 bundles, each worth fourpence. On 16 May 1620 Anne Stanley married Robert Rotton, whose family later occupied Home Farm. Probably the Stanley holding included Harborne Hall and Home Farm, and the trees cut down by Charles may have been on the Parkfields, near the church.

The Dudleys were in financial difficulties in the early 17th century, and began to sell their manors. Harborne and Smethwick first caught the attention of the Cornwallis family in 1604, and they increasingly gained control until in 1618 they bought the manor and, some say, came to live in Harborne. The local seat of the family was Blakeley Hall in Oldbury,

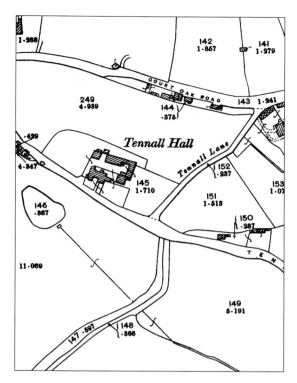

10 *Plan of Tennal Hall and surroundings in the late 19th century. (OS map 1900)*

11 *An impression of Tennal Hall in the late 19th century. It had been divided into two since at least the 17th century. (Based on photographs in the Donald Wright collection, Harborne Library)*

and Harborne representatives continued to attend courts there in the 18th century. The parish register also records the presence of members of the Paston family, whose Norfolk ancestors had written the famous Paston Letters. They had come to the Midlands because of their Cornwallis connections, the main seat of the Cornwallises also being in Norfolk.

12 *An extract from the parish register in 1698, showing the signature of the vicar, Richard Stubbings. (Parish register, held at St Peter's church, then at Birmingham Archives)*

During the civil war between Cavaliers and Roundheads, Harborne suffered in the same way as elesewhere. John Mackmath, the current vicar, wrote a Latin note in the registers, lamenting his inability to keep them as he wished. 'There are many things missing and unfinished here, as can be seen from the above entries. This is because the wickedness of men and the injustices of the times did not allow the real vicar to fulfil his duties.' Mackmath was a resident, as can be seen from the fact that his children were christened in Harborne. He is clearly upset that he cannot serve as he wishes. It seems that the villagers of Harborne took different sides in the war; a list made afterwards singles out Thomas Westwood and a small number of men from Smethwick as active Parliamentarians. Westwood was the tenant of 'Heathys House' in what is now High Street, roughly where the BP garage stands. Later members of the family sported strange biblical names, and it seems probable that Thomas was a Puritan. His relative, William Westwood, died in 1667 at his cottage in Tinker's Green. The Westwoods lost respectability and never again featured as part of the administrative gentry of the parish.

In 1653 a new register was begun. John Milward the younger was sworn as registrar and no longer recorded baptisms, but births. Marriages were performed at Hamstead Hall by Sir John Wyrley after due banns. Only burials continued in the hands of the church. These registers are fuller than the usual ecclesiastical ones, and record the names and occupations of the parents of the bride and bridegroom. Thus we learn of nailers and wheelwrights, husbandmen and yeomen, but mainly nailers. Clearly this occupation was far and away the most common in Harborne and Smethwick in those years, and was to continue so until the mid-19th century.

A major family in Harborne during the 16th and 17th centuries were the Birches. Their Smethwick branch held Holt Hill, near modern Roebuck Lane, while in Harborne Thomas Birch held a great deal of land including the area bounding Harborne Heath. The eldest Thomas Birch recorded in a register lived at Birchfield End in Handsworth, but later migrated to Erdington. It is not sure how he was related to the Birches of Holt Hill, but he chose one of them as godmother to his daughter Ann at her christening in 1584. Thomas was the father, in 1581, of a George Birch who became a tanner in Wolverhampton and left a great deal of money to his nephew Edward, in Northfield, a guardian of the Harborne Charity lands. George, who did not marry, was given his own apartment in the Harborne house of his brother Thomas. Altogether this first Thomas of Birchfield had 14 children. Several other Birches, including Thomas, were to the fore in administering the parish lands given by William Piddock and others, situated near the church, near Harborne Heath, and at Matchcroft, the triangle now occupied by St John's church and the All Electric garage. Another large area of parish land was subsequently used to build the workhouse in Lordswood Road.

A document which gives details of the Harborne population in the mid-17th century is the Hearth Tax, a way of extracting money from inhabitants according to wealth, judged by the number of fireplaces they had. There were 78 houses or cottages in Harborne proper on the 1666 list, many of which were exempted from payment. The

13 *An extract from the parish register in 1725, showing doodles by the non-resident vicar, Thomas Southall, after whose incumbency the parishioners determined to have a more local incumbent. (Parish register, held at St Peter's church, then at Birmingham Archives)*

minister, 'Mr' [Edward] Attwood, had two hearths in the vicarage. There were four or five larger houses, but most cottages had one fireplace only. The biggest house was that of Thomas Birch, with seven fires. This was probably 'the Manor House' at the top of later Fellows Lane, which was renovated in the 19th century and not

14 *The Manor House, Fellows Lane, at its demolition in the 1960s. It had been the seat of the Birch family when they were lords of the manor.*

15 *The Bell, near Harborne church. This old farmhouse was built in the 16th century, and the present building has parts from the 17th, 18th and 19th centuries.*

demolished until the 1960s. Thomas Milward senior lived at Tennal Hall, with five hearths, and Richard Baker probably at Harborne Hall. 'Mr' Charles Lane occupied an extensive house at later Poyner's Corner. Applying a well-known formula to obtain the total population of the Harborne part of the parish, we may guess the number of people was about 330; Harborne was still a tiny village. We can tell something about the occupations and lives of the people of Harborne at this

16 *Welsh House Farm in its latter days. This was perhaps a stopping place for Welsh cattle dealers.*

time by reference to their wills and the inventories of their goods made after they died. For example, Thomas Mucklow was a blacksmith who left about £18 after his unexpected death in 1666. His house had four rooms, a 'hallhouse' with a chamber over it, and a buttery, with a chamber also. He and his wife Elizabeth slept in a bed in the hall chamber, with little other furniture in the room. They ate at a table downstairs before a fire in winter with a pair of tongs to handle the wood, and a fire shovel. Over the fire they had pot 'geales' (variously spelt) to hang a cauldron for boiling water. There were hogsheads in the buttery and even two candlesticks. This is where they kept their five flagons and six pewter dishes. One blacksmith's shop at the time was near the southern end of Lordswood Road and this may have been Thomas Mucklow's.

A much larger house (perhaps newly rebuilt Harborne Hall) was the home of Thomas Baker, a yeoman with a sideline as a tailor. He left £255 and had 12 rooms in the house. One of the upstairs rooms is described as 'the painted chamber'. His tailoring took place in the 'little clossett' where he had five little boxes and tailoring tools. Thomas could read his Bible and his 'other small books', and in his kitchen he had stores of beef and bacon, with a pestle and mortar and a 'lanthorne' to see him through the dark days. His old house still stood nearby, with old bedsteads and an old tub waiting for disposal or renovation. Baker also had 'mucke' at the old house, worth £1 3s.4d. His crops had been successful the previous autumn, and he had £11 worth of barley and £12 10s. of pease and oats in store. He also owned a bull, with 12 cows, five heifers and four calves, four horses, five large pigs and eight small ones, and 17 sheep. On his pond he had some geese and there were hens in the yard. His heirs continued to live at the hall until the later 18th century.

17 *Cottage in Old Church Road. It has been renovated many times but was originally a farm cottage belonging to the Church Farm.*

A little before these inventories were taken, in 1661, the Cornwallises sold the manor to Thomas Foley, the son of the enterprising 'Fiddler' Foley, who is said to have brought home from Sweden details of a Swedish process for slitting iron to make nails. Thomas expanded his father's iron work and was able eventually to buy Witley Court in Worcestershire, where he lived the rest of his life. A friend of Samuel Pepys, he provided the diarist with a large iron box, locked with an ingenious key which Pepys could not find a way to open, but 'Jane the cook' could do so. He ceded part of his Harborne lands to his son Philip on his marriage to Penelope, the daughter of Lord Paget. It is possible that Penelope was being offered manorial rights which her father already claimed as lord of Longdon. The marriage settlement, dated 1670, included land at what is now Grove Park, with two

fields on the opposite side of Harborne Park Road, part of Home Farm, and some teritory near Lightwood (Lord's Wood) and Beech Lanes. Most of the field names are identifiable except for the strangely named 'Silly Greaves Rough'.

In 1671 Godfrey Ward took up residence as vicar of Harborne with his wife Jane and two daughters. He was a young man who had served his curacy and was now ready to take on a diffuse and poor parish. Jane gave him another daughter, Elizabeth, and then finally a son, Godfrey. After her death, Godfrey married for a second time, Mary. Her daughter Anne married Richard Bradley of Tennal Hall and Mary probably went there to live after the sudden death of Godfrey in 1696. Mary herself died nine years later, leaving £60 in her purse and what may well have been her husband's old desk. She had been used to ride, as is shown by the listing of a riding hood and saddle cloth. The most opulent inhabitant of Harborne at this time seems to have been Robert Rotton of Home Farm, who died in 1705 leaving more than £500. As well as Home Farm, where he had a flock of 30 sheep and 16 lambs, with 18 cows, a bull and 10 heifers, Robert farmed over the boundary at Selly Farm in Northfield. He had five sons living, Robert, Ambrose, John, Richard and Thomas, to share his inheritance.

FOUR

The Eighteenth Century
(1709-1790)

For centuries Harborne had been owned by absentee lords. This changed in 1709 when George Birch, who had lived in the farmhouse near the top of what is now Fellows Lane for some years, decided to buy the manor from Philip Foley. George was the great-grandson of Thomas Birch of Birchfield; some of his accounts and letters survive and show him to have been an energetic entrepreneur. He married Mary Foster from Castle Bromwich, who brought him a large sum of money, of which he acknowledges on paper the receipt of the first £500. He signalled the first rift between Harborne and Smethwick by negotiating a shared purchase with Henry Hinckley, Hinckley taking the Smethwick portion. It must be recalled that the Paget family of Beaudesert still exercised an overall interest, as theoretically Harborne was still part of the 'great manor' of Longdon. Deeds in the early 18th century therefore write of the area as 'called the manors and lordships of Harborne and Smethwick', setting aside a legal definition.

Hinckley and Birch agreed that the manors 'should be deemed to be divided by the common roadway that leads from Birmingham towards Halesowen' and that the boundary should be at the middle of the road. The documents relating to this purchase were put in a chest, to which George Birch had the key, in his 'dwelling in Harborne', the farm at Birches Green at the top of Fellows Lane. Hinckley was to be allowed all reasonable access. However, the villagers of Harborne and Smethwick became concerned about their rights over Lord's Wood ('Great Lightwood'). The custom was that after every 'fall' the wood should be enclosed for seven years for the trees to grow again. Now that George Birch had bought the southern part of the old manor, the commoners agreed that he should be allowed to 'enclose, plant, trench and improve' the woodland. It seems likely that some of the old oaks remaining from the wood in the area bounded by Hagley Road, Lordswood Road and Fitzroy Avenue were planted at that time.

The Birch family undoubtedly improved the administration of Harborne. Another benefactor was William Jephcott, who had originated at Anstey in north Warwickshire and had been a clergyman in Tardebigg. He owned the land once the property of Charles Lane: the area now covered by Crosbie Road, Wentworth Road, Londsdale Road, etc. He left in his will two legacies for Harborne and Birmingham residents.

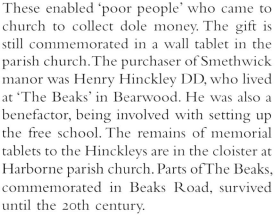

18 *The house of Samuel Pritchett in what is now Lordwood Road. This was the farmhouse for the Leyfield.*

19 *The golden cockerel placed on the top of the church tower in 1771. It was skilfully regilded in the 1960s.*

These enabled 'poor people' who came to church to collect dole money. The gift is still commemorated in a wall tablet in the parish church. The purchaser of Smethwick manor was Henry Hinckley DD, who lived at 'The Beaks' in Bearwood. He was also a benefactor, being involved with setting up the free school. The remains of memorial tablets to the Hinckleys are in the cloister at Harborne parish church. Parts of The Beaks, commemorated in Beaks Road, survived until the 20th century.

George Birch and his wife Mary produced seven children, all of whom survived. When George died in 1722 he left three farms in Erdington to his eldest son George, then of Henley-on-Thames, houses in Birmingham to James of Coventry, a property in Pedmore to Samuel, who was still at Pembroke College, Cambridge, and the residue to the second son Thomas, of the Inner Temple. Thomas was eventually one of the most distinguished residents of Harborne, becoming a Justice of Common Pleas and being knighted. Mary

Birch survived her husband for 11 years, dying in 1733. She left a very detailed will, passing most of her goods on to Thomas (then 'sergeant at law') with provision for John and James and also her daughter Sarah Green. She made arrangements for seven tenant farmers to draw her to church, for her body to be placed in a grave by her husband, and for funeral clothes, black gloves, etc., to be given to her servants. The pulpit could be hung with a cloth when the funeral sermon was preached. She also made provision for money to be given to the poor, and for legacies to her servants, John Hall, Anne Blackmore and Elinor Guest. The will shows her to have been a meticulous organiser, who evidently passed on some of her talent to her famous son.

Thomas, away in London, was now comfortable enough to marry. He chose Sarah Teshmaker, of Edmonton in Middlesex, already a rich and powerful woman. From this point on it seems that Thomas lived much of his time in London, exercising

20 *Charity board in St Peter's church recording the gift by Rev. William Jephcott of rents from land in what is now Crosbie Road, then part of a large farm.*

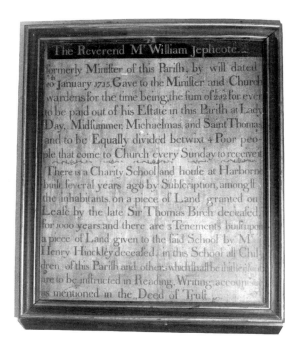

The Reverend Mr William Jephcote...
formerly Minister of this Parish, by will dated 20th January 1715. Gave to the Minister and Church wardens for the time being, the sum of £2,2 for ever to be paid out of his Estate in this Parish at Lady Day, Midsummer, Michaelmas, and Saint Thomas and to be Equally divided betwixt 4 Poor people that come to Church every Sunday to receive it. There is a Charity School and house at Harborne built several years ago by Subscription, among the inhabitants, on a piece of Land granted on Lease by the late Sir Thomas Birch deceased, for 1000 years and there are 3 Tenements built upon a piece of Land given to the said School by Mr Henry Hinckley deceased; in this School all Children of this Parish and others which shall be thither are to be instructed in Reading, Writing, accounts as mentioned in the Deed of Trust.

an influence on Harborne on his visits. The overseers of the poor in 1733 minuted an agreement that parish meetings should be held equally at Harborne and Smethwick until Thomas should come home; the agreement was ratified in front of two county justices, John Dolphin and William Pershouse. Thomas' marriage settlement gives a splendid catalogue of the manorial lands in Harborne, while the overseers' minutes show how once influential families had fallen on hard times. Like Tess' family in Hardy's novel, William Westwood now owned little: a pair of bedsteads, with their

21 *The* Green Man *at the Harborne Heath end of High Street. The present building replaced it just before the Second World War.*

22 *The former* Old House at Home. *This was further down Lordswood Road than the present building, and was previously a small farm.*

gear, three boxes, a brass kettle, an iron pot, a dresser, two barrels and a pail, and not much else. William lived at Tinker's Green (later the site of Yewdale in Harborne Park Road).

Just as Harborne had suffered from absentee manorial lords, so there had been difficulties over the clergy. It was usual in those days for vicars to hold more than one appointment, and they often preferred to live in Lichfield. Matters came to a head with the absence of Thomas Southall (whose curate, William Symmonds, was paid £20 p.a.), and after him the parishioners determined to have a local vicar. They influenced the

choice of Thomas Green, the usher at the Free School in Birmingham (King Edward's). He was a nephew of Joseph Green and quite probably linked with the Harborne family of that name. He proved a competent vicar, but inadvertently laid the ground for much later dispute by negotiating a composition for the tithes in 1737, details of which were evidently not committed to paper.

Earlier, a Smethwick resident, Dorothy Parkes, who had the interest of her native 'hamlet' in mind, was concerned about the neglect of the church at Harborne. When her sister Elizabeth Whiting died in 1718 her grave - in the church - was flooded.

23 *The cottage at Camomile Green (Queen's Park Road) occupied in the 1790s by the Firkin family. Ann Firkin was the sister of the squire, Thomas Green. The cottage was largely rebuilt in the 20th century.*

24 *Harborne Hall about 1800. This view is based on a drawing by a member of the Simcox family given to the Bishop of Birmingham in the 1920s. (Based on a contemporary drawing held first at Bishop's Croft, then Birmingham Archives)*

The grave had to be raised, and as a result the arch protruded above the floor of the chancel. Dorothy had the chancel floor relaid with 'ye better sort of quarrys' for better respect to the communion table. New communion rails were added at a cost of over £8. In 1721 Southall's salary was raised to £70 p.a. through an application to Queen Anne's Bounty, but the effect lasted only a short while. This story of a flooded church does not inspire confidence in its degree of sanitisation, considering that there were many bodies buried within its walls.

Dorothy Parkes also gave money for the poor of Harborne and Smethwick by an indenture of 1719, but her most significant step was to leave in her will £800 towards the building of a chapel for Smethwick ('Smethwick Old Church'). She left a further sum for the building of a school house near to the intended church. Dorothy possessed a great deal of land, including property at Titford and Warley Wigorn. Out of the rents she gave enough money to provide 'gowns' for three poor women of Harborne and three poor women of Smethwick each year. The names of the recipients for Harborne and Smethwick are recorded year by year in Smethwick register.

The fabric of the church itself was by now in poor condition. In 1752 it was decided to apply for money from neighbouring parishes to enable renovation to occur by means of a 'church brief'. It seems to have been at this time that the west end of the

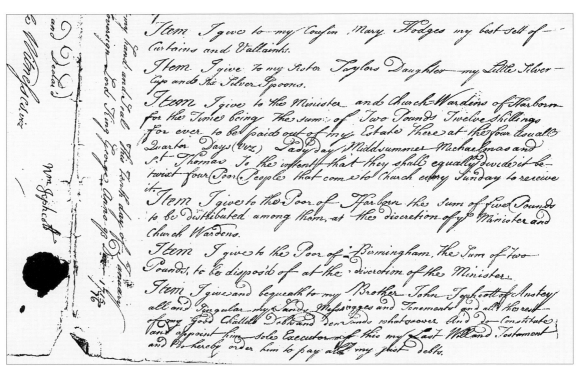

25 *An extract from the will of the Rev. William Jephcott mentioning his bequests to 'the Poor of Harborne' and 'the Poor of Birmingham', in addition to his specific bequest for poor people attending church to receive his dole.*

26 *Part of the inventory of Robert Rotton, who lived at Home Farm and died in 1705. The names of the rooms include the 'Man Servants chamber'.*

church was renovated with Georgian style windows and the top of the walls corbelled to take a new roof. It may have been at this time that the Hinckley memorial was shattered; it was evidently broken by the time the historian Stebbing Shaw tried to record it in 1798. The earliest remaining graves in the churchyard date from the latter part of the 18th century. The vicarage was also rebuilt at some time during the 18th century and attained the appearance it kept until the early Victorian rebuilding by J.T. Law. It seems that Thomas Green began acting as chief master at King Edward's from 1739, and used a house in New Street. Harborne vicarage was advertised to let. The advertisement described it as 'very near the Church, and two Miles distant from Birmingham; has four Rooms on a Floor, in very good Repair, convenient and pleasantly situated'. It had stables, a croft and a good garden attached. Thomas Green remained

vicar of Harborne until his death in 1766.

Parish officers at this time were elected annually to fulfil a number of functions, both for Harborne and Smethwick. A major task was the maintaining of the highways, which in a typical year (1757) cost £16 17s. It was hard to extract the taxes needed to do this job and to maintain the poor in and out of the workhouse in Lordswood Road. Landlords, especially such absentee gentry as the Pudseys, were continually defaulting, and the parish could not afford to take them to court. The parish accounts list paupers relieved and doctors' bills paid, e.g. to Dr Tomlinson in 1765 for his attention to Daniel Astley. One overseer of the poor, Job Freeth of Tennal Hall, travelled many miles round the parish on horseback. Legend tells that Freeth, a huge figure of a man, once fell off his horse near Tinker's Pool and caused a flood down in the valley at Harborne Mill.

27 *An impression of the 18th-century vicarage, based on a rough sketch in Birmingham Archives and a contemporary drawing at Birmingham Art Gallery. (Based on information from a contemporary drawing and sketches and plans in Birmingham Archives)*

28 *'Mill Lane' about 1800. This was the lower part of Harborne Park Road (the eastern carriageway) with the brook to the right of the road and a cottage, which had fallen into dereliction by 1827. The drawing is based on a sketch by Charlotte Price of The Park. (Interpretation of a drawing at Birmingham Museum & Art Gallery, with information on location and subsidiary features from Jacob's 1827 plan.)*

The old route route through Harborne via Gilhurst had been slowly giving way to the less hilly course via The Crossways (King's Head). In 1753 a turnpike trust was formed for the Hagley to Birmingham turnpike, passing through Harborne parish on the stretch between what is now Balden Road and the Chad brook. Gates were erected, the first gate at The Crossways being put up in 1759. This did not survive, and eventually the gate was nearer *The Dog* at the end of Lord's Wood. The first committee was honoured by the membership of the poet William Shenstone, who also had tenants in Harborne. The turnpike trust met frequently, making special rules for the passing of large numbers of cattle, and enquiring into nuisances, such as when Charles Brettle built a house near the *King's Head* obstructing part of the

road. Other important members of the trust were Jonathan Wigley of Ravenhurst and Hezekiah Green of Metchley Abbey.

In 1757 Sir Thomas Birch died, leaving his manor of Edmonton in Middlesex to his wife and most of the rest to his son George; this included Harborne. A related Thomas Birch, described as a yeoman, took over the farming of the lands at Birches Green, which covered the area round Fellows Lane, Court Oak Road and Beech Lanes estate. He and a number of associates were soon involved in a battle over the tithes, an everlasting source of conflict due to the inadequacy of the agreement negotiated by Rev. Thomas Green. The effect of this had been to commute the tithes into a money payment, called a modus. Because of the lack of clarity in the arrangement, in 1780 a legal dispute arose between Sarah Peach and William

29 *The foredraft to Welsh House Farm, roughly on the site of the present Fredas Grove.*

30 *The cedar tree in Grove Park, probably planted by Thomas Green, the new squire, about 1785.*

Colbourne, descendants of the Pudseys, and a number of Harborne farmers, including George Birch ('Esq'), Jonathan Wigley (of Ravenhurst), and James Poyner (of Poyner's Farm, based in what is now Vivian Road). The case was known as the 'hay modus' case. The enquiry sought to establish (i) whether twopence had been paid to the vicar for each 'Day's Math' of meadow grass and (ii) whether three halfpence had been paid for any other grass, not in water meadows. The farmers won the case.

During the 18th century there was a tax on windows. Very few of the documents survive, but one for Harborne made in 1784 gives an idea of the numbers of houses and their relative size. The largest was what later became David Cox's house in the Greenfield, then facing Heath Road (now High Street), though later the back and front changed places, so that the house faced Greenfield Road. This was tenanted by 'Bird and Barrs',

evidently manufacturers. The next largest were Upper and Lower Ravenhurst, with Jonathan Wigley and William Carless the tenants respectively. James Poyner's house had 12 windows, while the vicarage, the *Bell* (not so called) and Tithe Barn Farm each had eleven. Altogether there were 73 houses with windows to tax and for John Newey, with his Smethwick counterpart Luke Pope, to list.

For some years Thomas Green, a Birmingham manufacturer, had been making moves to gain control over land in Harborne. He was a son of Samuel Green and grandson of James Green, the miller at Harborne Mill. He is not to be confused with Thomas Green, the headmaster and vicar who had died in 1766. In 1781 he leased land in the centre of Harborne and began to build a new house on land called The Innage. This was to be Harborne House (later Bishop's Croft), and Thomas intended to live there and extend his influence in the village. In 1785 he bought the manor (of Harborne only, not Smethwick) from George Birch, who went to live at Hamstead Hall in Handsworth. Green also leased some of the last remaining open field land, in Greenfield. Over the last few years he had bought or leased almost all the manor land, and was in a position to become, in name and function, the squire.

Anxious to know the extent and value of his land, Green commissioned in 1790 a full survey. The map was drawn by Sheriff, a local maker of plans and surveys. This is the first known large-scale map of Harborne, showing each field and house on Green's 'manor' and giving the names of the holders of the rest of the Harborne lands. Green owned Harborne demesne, Harts Green Farm (now Church Farm golf course), Fieldhouse Farm, Church Farm (with farm buildings including the present cottage opposite the Roberts lych-gate; this was not the Church Farm of the golf course, but was centred on the *Bell*), Harborne Mill Farm, Bowling Alley (Metchley Lane), Wheets Farm (which had apparently been associated with the [*Golden*] *Cross*, and had no farm buildings), Grays Farm (Harts Green), and Fishers Farm (Harborne Hall). A major possession was the old Birch homestead, later called The Manor House,

with fields bounding Beech Lanes, also in Green's holding. Green also held Welsh House, Poyner's Farm and 35 cottages spread throughout the village, many on old waste land, with more on Harborne Heath. Only Weymoor and the area round Gilhurst, Ravenhurst and Hilltop were significant exceptions remaining outside Green's control.

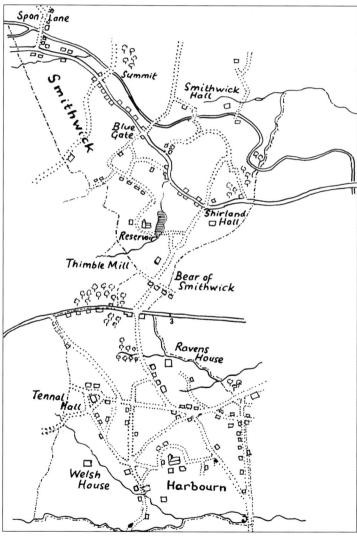

31 *Harborne parish (including Smethwick) in 1775. (Redrawn from Yates' map of Staffordshire)*

32   *Rectory Farm, later the verger's cottage and scout hut. Originally the farm belonged to the rector's glebe; in the 19th century this was one of the farms of the Tibbatts family.*

33   *Harborne House, now Bishop's Croft. This was built by Thomas Green in about 1780, before he bought Harborne Manor.*

34 *Former cottages in Lordswood Road, almost opposite Gilhurst ('Gillhurst') Road. They were renovated in the 19th century.*

There were many tasks for the new squire. He determined to educate the villagers by founding a new Sunday school. The year after he became squire this ambition was fulfilled, when he provided premises on his own land and the school started. (It did not affect the running of the free school, still located where All Electric garage now stands, under the doughty leadership of William Read.) A report on the new school made in 1791 shows that £85 4s. was being spent on salaries and £71 8s. 9d. on books. Another major expense was the fire in winter. The Sunday school, ostensibly religious, also provided a basic education in reading for children not attending the day school. In 1795 an appeal was issued to enable the school to enlarge its functions; among the contributors were the farmer Thomas Birch, William Tibbatts, William Green of Weoley Castle, and two relations of William Carless of The Ravenhurst, a Birmingham businessman, Mary and Anne Carless. Mary (born Prachett, of Bilston)

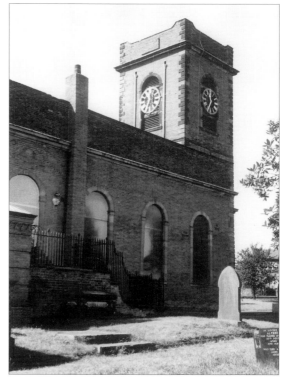

35 *Smethwick 'Old Church'. This was Dorothy Parkes' major gift to the parish of Harborne and Smethwick. It still has a rural, 18th-century feel.*

36 *Oak trees in Norwich Drive and Duncombe Close mark the 18th-century boundary of Lord's Wood.*

had married William in 1779, and they had three daughters: the eldest, Elizabeth, was to marry Thomas Attwood the reformer; Anne would marry John Freeman of Pedmore and become the mother of Edward Augustus Freeman; and Sarah remained unmarried. Mary Carless herself lived at The Grove and became the lady bountiful of the village.

The principal Harborne industry in the 18th century was nailing. The parish registers rarely give occupations, but burial entries from the 1750s and '60s sometimes mention nailers, labourers and husbandmen, while Simon Silke, buried 10 October 1762, is an 'awl-blade maker'. Harborne Mill, for long a corn mill, was for a time called Eacock's Mill. By 1767 it was involved in the making of metal parts of some sort (it is hard to discern exactly what), and at the end of the century it was a blade mill. Old illustrations of Greenfield House show a tall chimney, and in 1784 these premises were in the holding of Messrs Bird and Barrs, who paid £1 11s. 6d. for their 19 windows in the Window Tax of that year. Apart from this the industrial revolution had not yet impinged on Harborne.

It is hard to estimate precisely the population of Harborne during the 18th century. Putting together the evidence of the Window Tax and Sheriff's survey, it seems as though there was a population of six or seven hundred, including many children whose lives would be desperately short. However, the 1801 census shows 205 inhabited houses, with a total population of 1,178. Though numbers did grow in the 1790s, it looks as if there were more cottages than appear on the map. Some of these cottages, in very poor repair, would tumble down during the Napoleonic Wars; artists' drawings of the early 19th century show several in total decay. The whole village at this time was still primitive; it could have been as far from Birmingham as it was from London.

FIVE

The Parish Church and Vicarage

The oldest building in Harborne, still a major landmark, is St Peter's church, the original parish church of Harborne and Smethwick. Its medieval sandstone tower has dominated the view from the Hilly Fields for five hundred years. Standing in the wooded churchyard, surrounded by the graves of the 'rude forefathers of the hamlet', it provides a wildlife haven for woodpeckers and nuthatches, squirrels and frogs. But by the end of the 18th century, both church and vicarage were almost in a state of collapse.

At this time St Peter's church consisted of a single aisled building, with tower surmounted by a recently renovated weathercock. The south wall had two Early English windows, probably without stained glass, flanked by two circular windows. The south door had Early English features and there were two external buttresses on this wall. The west end had been rebuilt, and had a classical-style pediment above two 18th-century windows. The pediment was undecorated except for a small circular window. The north wall probably had five Early English windows, the two at each end being larger than the three in the middle. The tower had a gargoyle, and the tower windows were of a style dating

perhaps from the 14th century. There was a clock, which sometimes appears in the churchwardens' accounts. The west door had a surround which seems to date from the 15th century, leading to a vestry. The bells were those installed in 1691, and the churchyard had a paling fence around it. In 1803 the beadle was paid £1 6s. yearly and the ringers the same.

Traditionally the task of paying to keep the chancel (as well as the vicarage) in good repair devolved upon the owners of the great tithe. (The actual repair work was done by John Newey.) Earlier this had been the Pudsey family of Seisdon, but in the 1780s the tithe was paid to Samuel Peach, who had no interest in Harborne and had probably never been there; he had no wish to 'well and sufficiently repair uphold and maintain the chancel, barn and vicarage house'. This was despite the fact that his income from Harborne and Smethwick tithes was over £79 per annum, a considerable sum in those days. Neither the vicar, Richard Robinson, nor the curate, Robert Robertson, lived at the vicarage, and it was let to Joseph Tallis, workhousemaster. Robinson lived in Lichfield, and Robertson was the master of Halesowen School. Like Samuel Peach,

they simply milked Harborne. They were, however, nagged by the 'squire' Thomas Green and, after him, by the punctilious manufacturer, Theodore Price. This caused the engagement of James Clulee in 1807 as a carpenter to repair the ruinous vicarage and the farm at Smethwick. Twenty-one oaks, two ashes, two beech trees and two wych holms were sacrificed for this endeavour.

In 1813 Theodore Price took control of the churchwardens. Living at Harborne 'Park', he was near the centre of control. He sought to use some glebe land for a Sunday school, organising a visit from the Dean and Chapter of Lichfield for this purpose. He made a rough list of the pews in the church to try to sort out the rights of various parishioners to seating. Under his leadership, lists of the poor who came to receive 'bread money' and 'sacrament money' were kept from 1813 for ten years, and we are made

aware of how far the poor in the days of Napoleonic war and its following depression were kept alive by charity.

Still the old church festered away, with its muddle of wooden pews and uneven floor. It was by now too small for the growing population. However, it was not until the diocese decided to intervene, and Rev. J.T. Law was appointed vicar in 1825, that sweeping improvements could take place. The church would have to be enlarged and the vicarage partly rebuilt; Law intended to live there himself, at least for part of the time. An ex-military man, he set about a rigorous plan of updating facilities at Harborne. He called in a local contractor, Joseph Luckock, to repair the vicarage, and the architectural firm of Rickman and Hutchinson to enlarge the church. They gave the church its present floor plan.

Estimates were provided by Joseph Luckock for the vicarage improvements and for work at Smethwick (written 'Smerwick' in the document). The house was four square and built of local brick, with an attic, but had a coach house and laundry wing. It stood a little forward from where the modern vicarage stands but faced towards the church. Contemporary views show a pleasant rural garden in front. However, Luckock reported that the 'Wash house and Bedroom over it' were in such a ruinous state that they must be immediately taken down, and the coach house and laundry 'in a worse state'. He also proposed a new dining room, with bedroom and dressing room over, and that the washhouse should be taken down and rebuilt from scratch. In the event Luckock's plan was scrapped and a new vicarage was built, but not until the 1840s.

The state of the church can be deduced from a contemporary picture and Rickman's proposals. The medieval walls supported a low roof which made the interior dark. There was one aisle, and the diocesan visitors in 1825 were told that the average congregation was 280, sitting in box pews of all descriptions (one was so ugly and dominant that it was called 'the tank'). The west gallery housed the choir and the instrumentalists, and there was another small gallery on the north-east. There were graves under the floor. In 1798 the Staffordshire historian Stebbing Shaw claimed that the church had 'of late years' been rebuilt 'in a neat and commodious form', but this description certainly would not have been recognised by the

38 *A fanciful view of the church in snow, showing the avenue planted in 1833. The west end of the church is the one built in 1827 and demolished in 1867. (Based on a church Christmas card)*

parishioners. By this date Smethwick was the joint property of John Reynolds of Shireland Hall and John Baddeley of Albrighton, who also had land on the Harborne side of Hagley Road.

The main effect of the rebuilding in 1827 was to provide a south aisle 14 feet deep, with new wooden pews and an extended chancel, replacing the Georgian wall. Care was to be taken to use the old materials where possible, and to take down and re-erect the monuments, including those which can still be seen to Thomas Green's relatives, and to Robert Green and Hezekiah Green. The charity boards were retained and still

exist, but the brightly coloured coat-of-arms has disappeared. One monument which may have been there but is now lost is that to Thomas and Sarah Birch:

A greeabler couple could not be,
Whatever pleased he, always pleased she.

The tracery in the windows of the south wall was to be preserved and re-erected in the new building. For this, Rickman designed circular windows over the south porch and at the opposite end of the south wall, perpetuating the design of the earlier windows. The north wall and tower were unchanged. In the main body of the

39 *The church in 1842. (Based on a church Christmas card, deriving from a drawing by A.E. Everitt in the William Salt Library)*

40 *The church before rebuilding in 1867, from an early photograph. The north wall remains largely medieval, and the gargoyle can clearly be discerned.*

church, the old box pews remained. At this time new communion plate was bought, and is still in use every week. The older chalice was given to Smethwick at a later date. It is not clear what happened to the many bodies buried under the church itself. They may be still there, and, indeed, during alterations in the late 20th century a skeleton was found.

Some gravestones in the churchyard had to be moved; unfortunately, made of sandstone, many have not survived. Among those which are still legible are memorials to William Read the schoolmaster and John Tallis the parish clerk. Most of the really old graves cluster round the south-east corner of the church, under a venerable yew tree. One

grave which has now disappeared recorded the deaths of three successive husbands of one woman as follows:

This turf has drunk a window's tear,
Three of her husbands slumber here.

The three were John Clewes, died 5 August 1810, John Dean, died 6 December 1826, and Peter Parkes, died 8 July 1834.

The brick-built basement from 1827 replaced some graves and seems to have been retained in the later rebuilding. (An apparent opening at the east end does not lead to Metchley Abbey, as legend says.) The newly extended church was bigger but still dark because of the low ceiling. It certainly did not please the affluent merchants and manufacturers who were building their new houses in Harborne and expected dignity. The old instrumentalists gave way to an organ, but it was more remarkable 'for its old fashioned appearance than its sweetness of tone'. At evensong, each pew had a candle attached, but the light was so bad that the better-off brought lanterns with them. The position of the pulpit and clerk's box had been moved to the north aisle, with Samuel Dugmore, the local postmaster as well as parish clerk, occupying his seat after dropping the letters into the seat of each parishioner who had one.

Forty years after the church extension, it was decided to extend it again. Among those co-opted to plan the new building was Elihu Burritt, the American consul. An old picture in the church shows him and his fellow committee members in discussion, apparently in the old vicarage. The church would now become 'more imposing' and hold more parishioners. The Birmingham architect Yeoville Thomason was engaged, and prepared plans which can still be seen in the archives. It was his intention to retain the tower and north wall but clear out all the old box pews and replace them with neat rows of uniform pews. He added an apse and made the church cruciform by adding north and south chapels. It seems likely that the north wall crumbled as it was rebuilt, and it is impossible to tell how much of it remains in the fabric of the church today. Anything remaining was certainly faced in Victorian stone. The resulting nave was in essence a Victorian version of Early English style. Stained glass windows were part of the plan; the first was a memorial to William Westley Manning, dedicated on 28 October 1866.

SIX

The Early Nineteenth Century
(1800-1830)

The 19th century began under clouds from two major events: war with Napoleon and the 'industrial revolution'. The first had the effect of making government seek facts, and so led to censuses and accurate mapping. The second hastened the detachment of Harborne from Smethwick, while providing the money to build or enlarge mansion houses in Harborne itself. Methods of rating Boulton's internationally famed Soho foundry at Smethwick caused friction between the overseers of Harborne parish and Boulton in 1799. Village poor rates were not adapted to valuing and rating complex new industrial machinery, and Boulton proposed to appeal to the Quarter Sessions at Stafford for an assessment by reputable surveyors. The basis of his case was that other new factories in Smethwick were being assessed more favourably than his own. It is clear that the amateur parish officers could not cope with the demands of these new giant industrial complexes. However, a composition of some sort must have been agreed, because the case did not reach Stafford.

The first ever national census was held in 1801. No individual names are preserved, but there were 205 houses in Harborne proper, housing 219 families. An additional six houses were uninhabited. There were 585 males and 593 females, a total of 1,178. Of these, 95 people were involved in agriculture and 259 in trade, manufacture or handicraft. Most of them would have been nailers, though other small industries were taking their place, for example at the mill. (The overall population of Smethwick was slightly higher, at 1,284.) The ratio of working people to non-working (almost entirely small children) was 1:2.5. The figure of 205 houses seems large compared with the 73 on the Window Tax of 1784, but it must be remembered that many of these would have been so small as to obtain only little light.

Another effect of the industrial revolution was the pressure on communications. This had partly been ameliorated by the construction of the Dudley Canal from Selly Oak to Netherton, but much traffic had to go by the rutted, ill-maintained roads, and over bridges made for the Middle Ages. Though a sketch map of 1814 calls the present Harborne Park Road a turnpike, it was no such thing, and it issued in the narrow and decrepit bridge by the mill over the Bourn brook. The surveyors of the highways for Harborne, Edgbaston and Northfield met and decided a new bridge must be built, and it would be expensive.

None of their parishes separately could afford it, and a public subscription had to be set up. This route was vital to move manufactured articles from the northern side of Edgbaston, Smethwick and beyond, to the south west via Worcester.

Harborne's surveyors, Theodore Price and William Whitehouse, reported that the brook was a very dangerous water, and that the holloway leading from Selly Oak was equally so (the sharp hill still tempts drivers to exceed 30 m.p.h. here). There had been a number of accidents and 'one poor man, a waggoner, lost his life'. It was agreed that Northfield parish would make good the road from the bridge to Selly Oak, Edgbaston and Harborne would improve the road from the bridge to Five Ways (Metchley Lane), and Smethwick would renew Bearwood Road to the *King's Head*. Letters were sent out to potential subscribers for all this work, and subscriptions are recorded from 41 respondents. Among them were 29 Harborne residents, a few from Edgbaston and one each from Birmingham and Rowley. It is difficult to find any Smethwick names among the 'Harborne' contingent.

Two other places where roads required changes were the turnpike at Hagley Road and 'Poyners Corner' (Vivian Road). In 1808 the turnpike trust decided to erect milestones along this turnpike. The Harborne ones have disappeared, but one still stands between Five Ways and Highfield Road, Edgbaston. Improvements were also carried out by the vestry when Edward George Simcox gave land at the corner of Lodge Road and Park Lane (the corner of Vivian Road) to enable widening to take place here. The enlarged road was fenced and opened in 1833. In the same year the churchyard was enlarged and the avenue of trees from the rear of the church towards what is now Old Church Road was planted. More parochially, there were objections to the way in which Theodore Price dominated the parish. He and George Simcox of Harborne Hall had apparently made the old market road impassable by his plantation of trees (those at the bottom end of Grove Park and their successors) and put a gate at the top of what is now Grove Lane so that the church tenants could not get access to the glebe lands, the Bourne Hills (near the present *Hilly Fields* pub). These changes (called 'delapidations') were made in 1811 or 1812 so that the Hall would become more private. The market road was unused by this time and one suspects a power struggle between absent clergy and the powerful squirearchy. The tenant of the Old Farm (Grove House) at this time, perhaps the man most affected, was Benjamin Freeth (son of the great man Job Freeth).

Until this time there had been few terraces of cottages in Harborne. There was a row of four at the mill (later rebuilt as the row next to the present Harborne Mill petrol station), six or seven opposite the *Green Man*, and a small newly built terrace at Gravel Bank (later known as Crumpton's Cottages). In the next few years a spate of cottage building took place, enlarging Matchcroft, adding a row at Camomile Green, a row at Beech Lanes near the farmhouse, and Harborne Terrace, along the first part of High Street opposite Harrison's (Poyner's) Farm, on the south side leading from the *King's Arms*. (This terrace, which ended its life in the 1960s as a rather down-at-heel group of shops, had earlier been thought of

41 *The churchyard cottage, built in the 1830s, which became the residence of Samuel Dugmore and the original Post Office.*

as a group of capacious well-built houses.) Round the corner from these, Vine Terrace was built.

Many of these cottages were occupied by nailmakers, their nailshops at the back of the courtyard. These families had a rough reputation: Thomas Priest later records one woman at Camomile Green hitting her husband with a frying pan. The neighbours retaliated by making a 'Guy Fawkes' type effigy of the woman, and hanging it on an oak tree overhanging the lane. A young man boldly climbed the tree one night and cut the figure down. It fell on the head of a man called Tom Deeley, an old stoic, who merely said to the apparition falling on his head, 'Hallo'.

The village school was still located at the junction of High Street and Greenfield Road. In 1812 the long-serving schoolmaster William Read died, rather robustly calling himself a 'gentleman' in his will. He left some white and gilt china and a clock to his niece, and £10 to Elizabeth Baker, his sister. Her son Thomas Baker took over the role of schoolmaster, inheriting the house attached to the school. He was to retain his post for over twenty years and see the rebuilding on the same site of his school. However, this rebuild still failed to satisfy the growing population of Harborne and Smethwick, and by 1834 plans were afoot for a new school, the present St Peter's Junior. On retirement Thomas Baker claimed reimbursement for improvements to the old school, a new pump, a partition in his house, iron grates in the kitchen, a copper furnace and an iron boiler; he would be leaving at midsummer 1834. His grave in the churchyard, near the path to the front door, records that he died the next year.

During his years as schoolmaster, Thomas Baker, like his uncle before him, had been the scribe for the village. He wrote letters for everyone, helped the illiterate to make their wills, doctored their families and inoculated them for cowpox. His ex-pupils came to him with legal queries and he sorted out disputes. He subscribed to charities and, with Joseph Tallis, remembered old customs and field names. He made a bridge between

gentry and villagers, and was not forgotten after his death. He helped to found an old Harborne institution, the Gooseberry Growers' Society, in 1815. In the fullness of time this helped to make Harborne famous throughout Staffordshire.

The wealthy squire, Thomas Green, died in 1803, leaving an estate worth thousands of pounds. His permanent legacy to Harborne was the stately Harborne House (Bishop's Croft). He left most of his land and money to his sons-in-law Theodore Price and George Simcox. The Simcoxes received most of the land on the western side of the manor, from Harborne House through Fellows Lane and Camomile Green to Beech Lanes, while the east went to Theodore Price, whose 'park'

42 *The schoolmaster's house, built in 1837 and renovated in the 20th century. Its cottage style echoes that of the original schoolhouse on High Street.*

gives its name to Harborne Park Road. The last member of the Birch family, widow Sarah, was allowed to spend the final part of her life in the Manor House at the top of Fellows Lane. Price's part of the legacy covered many frontages in High Street, and would later be enormously valuable as these were developed.

Thomas Green left his sister Ann Firkin, living in the cottage by Camomile Green, £20 p.a., and put Mary Carless of the Grove (widow of William Carless of Ravenhurst) in charge of £20 to be spent on the poor. He made careful arrangements for his own funeral, providing mourning clothes for the curate, the beadle, the assistant Sunday school teacher, and Samuel Pritchett the singing instructor. Thomas's brother, Hezekiah at Metchley Abbey, died five years later in financial difficulties brought about by the war with Napoleon, leaving to Phoebe his wife his goods and effects, 'though God knows [they] are now very trifling'. His will was not properly attested, but it was accepted. Later, Metchley Abbey passed into the hands of the Freeman family, relatives of the Carlesses. A blue plaque records the birth here of E.A. Freeman, who dominated Victorian historiography. Metchley Abbey itself was rebuilt and extended about this time. There are no early pictures of this mansion, but the west wing may have been Elizabethan; however, most of the house dates from the early 19th century.

Many years later a descendant of Thomas Green, Jane Margretta Simcox, wrote down her memories of early life at Harborne House. In the 1820s this well-off family was continually plagued by deaths; their joys were always short-lived. For six months in

43 *'Murphy Row': Vine Terrace. The original houses were built in the 1820s; the front house was rebuilt in the 20th century as a replica and the rest were demolished.*

her childhood Jane was kept in her room with inflammation of the lungs; the cure was to have leeches applied to her chest. Her mother died of typhoid in 1826, and her father two years later. On Ash Wednesday 1828, 'we knew we were orphans'. There had been many interesting activities in her childhood: cutting out clothes for the poor which the children took to their cottages; running along the corridor at the top of the house playing Blind Man's Buff, or games with the rocking horse and dolls. She records a large party of tenants and friends singing sacred songs before supper and comic ones

44 *The village schoolmaster, Thomas Baker, who died in 1835. His grave, with those of his relatives, is in Harborne churchyard. (Originally in Presterne,* Harborne Once Upon a Time, *copy in Harborne Library)*

afterwards. Charles Hemus, tenant farmer at the Manor House, sang 'The Spinning Wheel' and 'The Old Beggar Man', and everyone burst out laughing. She did not know, as we do now, that the whole manor of Harborne was mortgaged in 1822.

Jane Margretta was very fond of the Harborne House garden, which included the large walled garden with its oval lawn, toolshed and hot house. Here grew both black and white grapes, while on the walls in the garden grew peaches, apricots and nectarines, with espalier apples trained on each side of the path. Outside the garden was the large field, in which the boys flew kites and shot stones from home-made slings. In summer, the children played on the hayricks, 'a source of happy play and merriment'.

If even this apparently rich family had its tragedies, for the poor it was much worse. After the war money became tighter and both rich and poor suffered. The workhouse, shared by Harborne and Smethwick, was governed by Joseph Tallis, who also kept a

45 *The workhouse for Harborne and Smethwick before the 1834 Poor Law. It was later called 'High Harborne'. The yew tree in the picture is now much larger, and the workhouse has been demolished.*

46 *Restored version of the grave of John Tallis, for thirty years parish clerk of Harborne, who died in 1797. This sandstone grave is now very worn. (Restored from photographs by the author, checked with information from the parish registers)*

47 *Memorial of the Tibbatts family recording deaths of their children and of Mrs Mary Tibbatts, who died in 1817. The grave is now worn. (Restored from photographs by the author, checked with information from the parish registers)*

public house, *The Maypole*, where Church View now stands. The workhouse site had been chosen as halfway between the centre of Harborne and the beginning of Smethwick, and the house had been rebuilt. When Tallis died in 1833, his wife Sarah took on the role of governess. There was dissension among the workhouse guardians when one of them accused the others of 'feasting and drinking' on the premises. There was much temptation to do so, as they had just survived the terrible cholera outbreak of 1832. Harborne was quite fortunate in suffering much less than other parishes in the neighbourhood, but this probably had little to do with the setting up on 26 December 1831 of a committee dividing the parish into five small areas to take necessary precautions. So far as can

be understood, these generally consisted of using whitewash on grimy buildings; no one knew then that cholera was water-borne.

Some poor (but deserving!) children could escape from the drudgery they would otherwise face by gaining nomination to a free place at Oldswinford Hospital School in Stourbridge. The vestry sat once a year to consider their applications. It seems possible that this contest was biased in favour of Harborne and against Smethwick, as Thomas Baker rejected Henry Newby, son of a Smethwick carpenter, out of hand in 1834 on the grounds that he had not been baptised until 1828. George Smallwood, son of Noah the gunloop maker in Metchley Lane, was one of the Harborne candidates, with Thomas Hart, a plater's son, Henry

48   *Metchley Abbey, home of Edward Freeman, the Victorian history writer. The original building was an ordinary farmhouse, as can be seen from the left-hand gable.*

49   *The foredraft to the old Rectory Farm, later the verger's cottage. On the left is the high wall of Harborne Hall.*

Richards, son of a nailer, George Evans, the blacksmith's boy, William Soden, John Hadley, son of a small farmer in Smethwick, George Richards from a nailing family, James Stevens, a farmer's son from the *Bell*, and James Harrison from the Mill Farm. From these Thomas Hart and James Harrison were finally chosen. It cannot truthfully be said that James was from a poor family, as his father tenanted a viable farm.

On his accession to the vicarage at Harborne the new Lichfield-appointed vicar J.T. Law found it difficult to discover how much poor rate should be paid, and indeed who owned what land. He decided to commission a new survey of the whole parish, including Smethwick, to be undertaken by a qualified surveyor, H. Jacob of Birmingham. Late though it is, this is the first detailed plan of the whole parish. The work was undertaken in 1827, and the plan shows new houses built in the early years of the century. It records many known field names, but suggests that Jacob was not very diligent in this aspect of his work, since many older names are preserved in the Harborne Overseers' Book of 1859. However, Jacob did make plans of all the houses and other buildings which existed in both north and south parts of the parish.

Another major matter of concern to Law was the distance from the church of the village school. He determined it would be brought closer to his oversight, so that the children could be brought into church for various activities. In this he was successful, and the closeness of St Peter's Infants' and Junior schools to the church today means that the clergy can be involved in the children's education. Part of Broad Leasow, manorial land, was set aside for the new school. The

50 *The grave of William Read, schoolmaster at the 'free school' for 49 years. (Restored from photographs by the author, checked with information from the parish registers)*

design replicated the earlier brick and stone cottage appearance of the earlier school and the jewel is perhaps the original headmaster's house, still standing, and looking out over a playground which is the same area as it was when the school first opened in 1837. A new head was sought and found in Samuel Bradley, who was assisted by the mistress, Sarah Astley. Bradley was known for his firm discipline, keeping order in church by hitting the boys on the head with a long stick capped with a bone knob. Later in the century very young women were assistant mistresses, including the daughter of Samuel Dugmore, the village registrar and postmaster.

By this time directories of better-off citizens were being published. Among these were *The Staffordshire General and Commercial Directory* of 1818 and Pigot and Co.'s *National Commercial Directory* of 1835. The former includes the names of Joseph

51 *A 19th-century house in Lordswood Road, nearly opposite Knightlow Road. It was demolished in the 1960s.*

52 *Title page of the rules for the Girls' Friendly Society, 1827.*

RULES AND ORDERS,

TO BE

OBSERVED AND KEPT,

BY

THE MEMBERS

BELONGING TO THE

Female Provident

SOCIETY,

HELD AT THE HOUSE

OF

JOHN NEWEY,

SIGN OF

THE OLD KING'S ARMS,

HARBORNE.

"Love as sisters,
Relieve the distressed,
Plead for the widow,
Be kindly affectionate towards each other."

BIRMINGHAM:
PRINTED BY T. AND W. WOOD, 78, HIGH STREET.

1827.

Tallis, 'governor of the house of industry' (the workhouse), Thomas Baker, schoolmaster, two 'Tibbitts', farmers, and two publicans, William Gray of the *Nag's Head* (*King's Head*) and John Westwood of the *Green Man*. The 1835 directory subsumes Harborne residents under Birmingham, together with Edgbaston and Handsworth. Among the Harbornites listed are James Thomas Law and Thomas Attwood, perhaps the most famous Harborne resident in the early part of the 19th century. He had been born at Hawne in Halesowen in 1783, and his first known association with Harborne was in 1806 when he married Elizabeth Carless. A banker in partnership

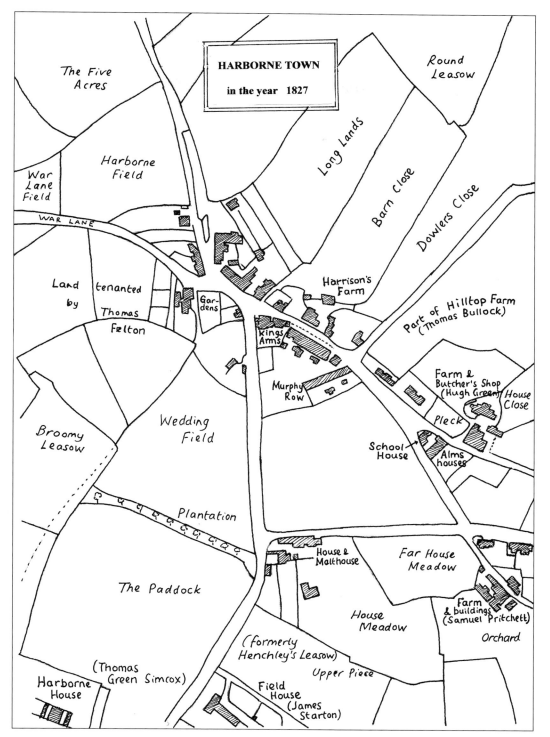

The Five Acres

HARBORNE TOWN

in the year 1827

Round Leasow

War Lane Field

Harborne Field

Long Lands

Barn Close

Dowlers Close

WAR LANE

Land tenanted by Thomas Felton

Gardens

Harrison's Farm

Part of Hilltop Farm (Thomas Bullock)

Kings Arms

Murphy Row

Farm & Butcher's Shop (Hugh Green)

House Close

Pleck

Wedding Field

School House

Alms houses

Broomy Leasow

Plantation

The Paddock

House & Malthouse

Far House Meadow

Farm & buildings (Samuel Pritchett)

House Meadow

Orchard

(formerly Henchley's Leasow)

Upper Piece

(Thomas Green Simcox)

Harborne House

Field House (James Starton)

53   *Plan of the village in 1827, based on Jacob's survey, with information added.*

54 *The original* Vine Inn. *It was built in the 1830s.*

out to pull him home in his conveyance, substituting for horses. On the traditional 'heaving day' (Easter Tuesday) some women met him out walking. It was usual on this day for women to heave the men in the air three times and ask for a kiss and a 'silver forfeit'. The village women told Attwood, 'Now we'm a-goin' to heave yer.' Attwood's reply was, 'No, ladies, don't heave me, but here is a five pound note.' The women went away very pleased! Attwood lived at the Grove until 1846, when he moved south for health reasons.

A social enterprise founded in 1812 was the Harborne Friendly Society, with its meeting place at the *King's Arms*. This was an elementary form of social security to supplement the charity and church organisations. Any members who died or fell sick would have their dependants looked after. The rules of the society were strict, with penalties for swearing, playing cards or dicing. Each first Monday in May (the society anniversary), the members' children had a holiday from school and walked to church dressed in Sunday best, with a light blue sash and a silver medal. They were preceded by the banner, and the sight was described as 'very pretty', with the village band leading the procession in triumph. A women's version followed in 1827.

with Abraham Spooner, he moved to The Grove in 1823. At this time Birmingham had no parliamentary representation, and there was great need for reform. In 1830 Attwood was instrumental in forming the Birmingham Political Union, an idea which was quickly adopted in other parts of the Midlands and elsewhere. Attwood's aim was peaceful reform, and he organised marches and gatherings to this end. After two attempts, the First Reform Bill was passed and Birmingham enfranchised. Attwood became one of Birmingham's first two MPs.

Attwood was a hero in his own village. On his return from London villagers ran

SEVEN

Early Victorian Harborne

The nation was about to change, and in the change the Birmingham area would be crucial. The shift from sleepy villages to complex industrial conurbation gathered pace in these years. Almost as soon as Victoria had ascended the throne, a bill was passed to rationalise land use and taxation, shifting the emphasis of tax from crops and flocks to land use: the Tithe Commutation Act. In the case of Harborne this entailed a new survey, field by field and house by house: the Tithe Award and Map. Carried out between 1838 and 1843, the survey is supplemented by the first census which collects all names and ages, giving us a record of each household in the country: the 1841 census. One of the aims was to find out the trades of the people in every parish in the country; another was to discover how many immigrants, Irish and others, were living in England.

For the tithe survey in Harborne a Scotsman named David McFarlane was chosen. He had an apprentice, Hugh Stowell Brown, and because of the wet and cold encountered in their surveying they often spent time in public houses during their previous survey in Shropshire. They were awarded the contract for Harborne in the freezing January of 1840, travelling to a 'forlorn' Birmingham, with its ragged and half-starved workmen standing on street corners. They were to live in Smethwick while they surveyed the parish. The intention was to rework Jacob's 1827 map and, because they were not starting from scratch, the pair had taken on the work at a cheap rate. Arriving in Smethwick, McFarlane soon saw that the work he had expected to take a month would take four, because of the large number of new buildings erected since Jacob's survey 13 years before. Hardly sober when he reached Smethwick, McFarlane realised he had better mend his ways, and did so. The work was very hard in that bitter winter for his 15-year-old apprentice, who would be tramping through muddy streets and fields all day. However, the plan they eventually produced appears reasonably accurate, showing every house and farmyard.

Samuel Dugmore was chosen as enumerator for Harborne census. Living in the churchyard cottage (still existing, opposite the Roberts lych-gate), also the post office, he knew many residents, and certainly could find his way round the village, along back lanes and farm tracks. He began his investigation at the *Green Man*, asking the names of all the residents in each house, their ages and occupations, and whether or not they had been born in Staffordshire. Adults were allowed to round down their ages to the nearest five years, but children below fifteen gave their exact age. From the *Green Man*, the route lay down Metchley Lane, taking in Noah Smallwood, the gun loop

maker whose son George, now 17, had been an unsuccessful candidate for Oldswinford Hospital in 1834. George was the oldest boy at home, helping his father in the workshop. Next to this house was William Farmer, shoemaker, and then three more families, among whom Thomas Freeman was an

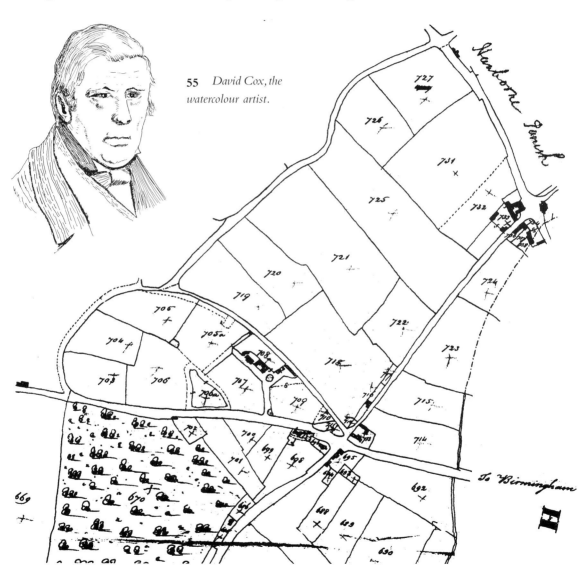

55 *David Cox, the watercolour artist.*

56 *The King's Head and Bearwood, from the Tithe Plan of 1840. Lightwoods House, the* King's Head *pub and the* Bear Hotel *are all shown. The junction is now called King's Head Cross.*

57 *An outhouse from Victoria Road, built in 1857, showing small industrial windows. Like many 19th-century properties, this house originally had its own well and pump.*

agricultural labourer (though by 1851 he had become a button cleaner). Along the rest of this part of Metchley Lane lived a plater, a forger, a gilt toy maker and William Kempster, military ornament maker. Metchley Abbey, the strange Gothic building which had once been a farmhouse, was now the home of an ironmaster, Charles Birch. He was a close friend of his neighbour, David Cox, and an authority on paintings. During his time the abbey (also called 'Harborne Abbey') was kept in good repair.

Theodore Price's land was almost adjacent, and beyond this two small farms kept going: Mrs Allen's and that of Mrs Sarah Fulford, whose husband William she reported as alive for the census although he had died the year before. Near the mill, Benjamin

Cleary kept the *Cross* (now the *Golden Cross*). He had come to Harborne from Charlbury in Oxfordshire on his marriage. He gave lodging to John Humphries, an agricultural labourer and illegitimate son of the pauper Catherine Humphries. John's sister Ann made little progress at school though she stayed much beyond the normal time. In 1834 she is recorded as living at the workhouse, but died two years later and was buried on 28 September 1836. The mill was at this time a wire mill, engaged in drawing steel into wire. The Mill Farm (origin of Mill Farm Road) was run by James Harrison, former maltster and horse dealer, whose son had been successful in the Oldswinford School competition. A new occupation appearing at this time was that

58 *David Cox's home, Greenfield House, Greenfield Road. Originally the house faced what is now High Street.*

59 *The original Wesleyan Methodist church in High Street, which later became the Catholic school, and then shops.*

of potato dealer, and we can assume that some smaller fields and gardens were planted with potatoes, which would be taken into Birmingham market for sale to the ragged and emaciated poor whom McFarlane's apprentice had noticed.

The rich area of Harborne clustered round the rural church was home to Edward Cresswell, another ironmaster, who lived in Harborne House. George Simcox's widow Elizabeth lived at the hall, with three female servants to look after her. John Tibbatts farmed the rectory farm, while the schoolmaster Samuel Bradley lived in the new schoolhouse, and the *Harborne Tavern* was kept by Joseph Stokes, a former

painter and glazier from Birmingham. Lady Charlotte Law was at home in the vicarage on census night with her four children. We can assume that J.T. Law had been called away on business, probably to Lichfield. There were no fewer than six servants at the vicarage to look after this family. Finally, in this small community, Benjamin Stevens kept the *Bell* with his six children and one nephew to help with the market gardening aspect of the pub.

The further west in the parish, the more nailers. There was a small group of them at Harts Green and even more at Gravel Bank. Camomile Green had seven nailing families, almost all of whom were born

60 *Cottage Row, sometimes called 'Matchcroft Cottages', built in the 1840s. The original Matchcroft cottages were on the library site next door.*

61 *A panorama from the Clocktower looking west. South Street Methodist church can be seen in the middle distance, and on the horizon the row of poplars by the Grove.*

62 *St John's Road, so named after the original St John's church, built in the 1850s. The church, opposite this house, was destroyed by a bomb in the Second World War.*

63 *Houses at the bottom of Vivian Road, built at the same time as 'Cottage Row' in the 1840s. They were demolished and the site is now Safeway car park.*

in Harborne. These three hamlets, with their cottage rows, were typical small Black Country communities, whose roots in the region went back for many generations, as the names of Westwood, Deeley, Smallwood, Rose and Cutler show. Behind the cottages were nailshops, where the little Joseph Deeley (10), Harriet Smallwood (8) and Jesse Cutler (10) would do their fair share of making nails out of the nailrod brought home by father the week before. The large farms in this area were as productive as ever: Tennal Hall (farmed by Joseph Pearman), Harts Green (farmed by John Rutter) and, best of all, the Home Farm, farmed by the well-off William Lea, with his two agricultural labourers (one from Aston Cantlow in

Warwickshire) and two young servant girls. Lea also farmed land on the Northfield side of the brook, in Bartley Green.

Turks Lane is the old name for Queen's Park Road. The Turk in question was old Abraham Westwood, a man of 'gipsy-like' appearance, who did carrying and carting. After his death his descendants Enoch and Joseph continued his eccentric tradition. They went in for biblical Christian names: Simeon, Isaac, Reuben, Emanuel and Keziah. The family were always in and out of the charity books, and Ann Westwood went by the nickname 'Nanny Mo', because she was Moses Westwood's daughter-in-law. Beyond their houses was the 'miser's cottage', the home of George Downing, a landowner

64 *Chemical retorts from Albright and Wilson, used as walling in Steampot Lane, which once ran across what is now the municipal golf course. There is more of this walling at the top of War Lane.*

65 *Metchley Lane: the house of Daniel Richards in the 1840s.*

who normally went about in rags and was said to have gold stored under the bed. On Sunday he dressed up and marched in military fashion through Camomile Green on his way to church.

At the end of his round, Samuel Dugmore added up the figures (we still have his calculations, in his own handwriting) and found that there were 302 inhabited houses, with 796 males and 841 females, making a total of 1,637 people in Harborne proper. He had covered three enumeration districts, and completed his summary on 27 June 1841, taking the results to the Superintendent Registrar, Joseph Woodward, on 7 July. Of these houses, only a scattered few remained to greet the 21st century.

The development of Smethwick, which so alarmed David McFarlane, was of concern to the patrician family of Simcox. Thomas Green Simcox, grandson of George, born in Harborne in 1810, became curate

66 *The pool on Metchley Grange estate; the area below it was once called Botleys.*

67 *The Harborne Railway bridge over Park Hill Road. Threatened with demolition, it was saved after protests led by the Harborne Society.*

68 *Alma Passage in the 1960s, looking towards High Street. The trees in the background are on land now occupied by MFI.*

at St Peter's in 1833. He bought land in the centre of Smethwick from John Unett and built a new church. This church, Holy Trinity, North Harborne, was consecrated in 1839. To it he added a parsonage in 1839 and church schools in 1840. His obituary claimed that he played ' no small part in the progress and destiny of the modern borough of Smethwick'.

In 1841 the Birmingham–born water-colour artist David Cox came to live in Greenfield House. He soon settled down to a routine of painting in the morning

69 *Tibbets Lane, named after the Tibbatts family who tenanted Tithe Barn Farm, now Church Farm golf course. The family name has been spelt in various ways.*

70 *Victorian towers on private houses at the north end of Albert Road.*

and again in the afternoons, with his local friends, Charles Birch and William Roberts coming in during the evening for discussions. It was from this house that he made his expeditions to the Welsh hills. Charles Birch painted his portrait (in Birmingham Art Gallery) in 1856, and by this time the master was ailing, having had a slight stroke in 1853. He fell ill with bronchitis in July 1858, and is said to have bade a half-humorous farewell to his own paintings on his way to bed on the 6th. On the morning of 7 July he died, and was buried in Harborne churchyard, where his grave may still be seen. He had been a good neighbour and a philanthropic citizen. In 1851 he had given £2 to the poor, depositing it in Taylor and Lloyd's bank for their use until it was all gone. Doubtless he had been moved by the poverty at the other end of Greenfield Road, where the Snuggery, partly a decrepit

71 *The Birmingham Civic Society plaque on David Cox's house in Greenfield Road.*

old medieval building, was inhabited by nailers and men out of work

Certainly the poor were a constant problem at this time. The Harborne Charities (now Harborne Parish Lands) were dealing continually with sad cases like Marianne

72 *Harborne Vicarage, demolished in the 1960s.*

Bramwich, 'her husband a higgler, badly off and struggling', to whom they gave 5s. to see her through. At the same session Daniel Richards, 'old and sick', was given 2s. 6d. and 'Blind Richards' the same amount. Elizabeth Parry had a sick child; she was given 2s. 6d. for wine and arrowroot. And the widow of Edward Harrison in Fish Lane was given 3s. for her own illness, her husband being out of work.

The official system for the relief of the poor had now changed, so that larger areas than the parish were responsible for them. Harborne and Smethwick became part of Kings Norton Poor Law Union, whose workhouse was to be at Selly Oak, now Selly Oak Hospital. The Harborne overseers were still responsible for collecting taxes (for both Harborne and Smethwick), however, and passing the revenue on to Selly Oak. Revenue was still based on houses and farmland, rather than industrial property. Their inventory for 1859 shows such places as cowhouses, stables, gighouses and gardens, but nailshops seem to be called just 'premises', although John Newey has 'house, workshop, stable, sheds, timber yard, etc.' This tax schedule perpetuates a surprising fact from the 1841 and 1851 censuses, no individual name being given to the largest farm in Harborne, the land now called Home Farm.

EIGHT

The Later Nineteenth Century (1860-1887)

By the 1860s Birmingham had become a prosperous manufacturing town – a city in all but name. Expansion north-west and southwards began to engulf Handsworth and Balsall Heath. Expansion south-westwards was harder, except in houses for the very rich, since the Calthorpe Estate covered most of Edgbaston, and on this there was no enthusiasm to house clerks and silversmiths. The answer was to leap over Edgbaston and begin to build on plots in Harborne. After the development of Bull Street, York Street and what was originally to be Josiah Street (now South Street), more land became available in Metchley Lane, Lodge Road (Vivian Road) and the High Street. Most of this was sold by the squirearchy, the Simcoxes and the daughters of Theodore Price, Charlotte and Laura, both of whom retired to Tunbridge Wells, where Charlotte died in 1869 and Laura in 1887. During their residence at The Park, Charlotte made sketches of contemporary Harborne scenes.

In 1860 Samuel Dugmore was still running the post office, where letters arrived by mail cart from Birmingham twice a day. The last collection in the evening was 8 p.m., much later than today! Village life was dominated by a new group of manufacturers, not all of local origin. In this they mirrored the new residents of recently developed terraces. The Hall was occupied from 1856 to 1867 by William Roberts, a Yorkshire metal merchant and amateur artist. Thomas Millington used the mill premises to make steel plate and lived at his newly built Dore House in Lordswood Road. This was named after the village near Sheffield where his wife had been born (it has since acquired an acute accent on the final E).

By now Harborne had sufficient wealthy residents to be able to set up celebrations on a grand scale. In March 1863 there were major festivities when the Prince of Wales married Princess Alexandra. Humbler entertainment was provided by the skittle alley at the back of the *King's Arms*, where skilled and 'good tempered' men competed in front of long rows of spectators, coppers and sixpences being placed as small bets on the result. The *King's Arms* was the social as well as the physical centre of the village in those days. About this time the present Gothic building (but without the half-timbering) replaced the 17th-century public house.

An influential resident in the later 1860s was the American 'consul' in Birmingham, Elihu Burritt, who lived at what is now 11 Victoria Road. His book, *Walks in the*

73 *Elihu Burritt, the American 'consul' in Birmingham, who wrote the first book on the Black Country.*

Black Country and its Green Borderland, is well known and has been reprinted. He records looking out from his western window towards Clent, and claims that the Harborne resident can enjoy evening scenery which is unique and even grand, with the sky providing 'its own aurora borealis' running down the horizon like summer lightning; this is 'the halo round-the brow of sweat and patient labour'. We might think this a romantic view of foundry and forge life, if it were not that Burritt was known himself as the 'learned blacksmith'. After his death a poem was written about him by the local poet Alfred Smeaton Johnstone.

Thomas Short, ironmaster, lived at Clent House in Harborne Park Road (the entrance gate pillars still stand). He used to ride to Birmingham in a phaeton, offering lifts to the villagers. Most people walked the

74 *Elihu Burritt's house in Victoria Road, from the rear. This picture shows the great man enjoying a rest in his back garden. (Based on a magazine article discovered by Donald Wright)*

75 *Clent House, on the corner of Harborne Park Road and St Peter's Road. The gateway still exists, though the house was demolished in the 1960s.*

76 *A view of the* King's Arms *and High Street, showing the public house after rebuilding in the late 19th century.*

three miles to town, travelling by 'Long Lane' (Harborne Road), which at times of religious tension had graffiti such as 'No Popery' daubed on the walls. Another ironmaster, David Jones, lived at Harborne House, but his wealth did not save him from illness and he rarely if ever went to church, making sure instead that his family did so. On the death of William Roberts, in 1867, Charles Hart took up residence in the Hall. A wrought iron manufacturer, he and his family were to be influential. He did not give his name to Harts Green, which was

77 *The 'Hart' lych-gate. Of the three lych-gates, this is the oldest. (Based on a photograph of a painting in the side chapel at St Peter's church)*

78 *Albert Walk, popularly known as 'The Stumps'. It was here that one of the field paths from the church entered the village streets.*

79 *Brighton Terrace: Victorian infill which closed the gap between the original village ('Harborne Town') and the houses on Heath Road (now High Street.)*

so called many years before, but perhaps he was descended from the Harborne Harts. He was born in London, and the year after he arrived he gave the church its first-lych gate; inscribed with his name, it is still standing. The brass eagle lectern in the parish church was also his gift in 1874. South of the Hall and Harborne House, Park Lane (Harborne Park Road) boasted large mansions such as Woodcote, Englefield and Yew Dale (the name perpetuated in modern flats).

Thomas Short's phaeton was not always available for Harbornites to travel to Birmingham. In any case, the roads were dirty with horse manure (and mothers would say to their children, 'keep out of the horse road'). At the *Duke of York* end of the High Street, William Astley, the village blacksmith, plied his trade in a thatched forge next to the *King's Arms*. Railways were the modern method of travel, and in 1866 a Harborne Railway Company was formed and authorised to build

80 *Harborne's best-known landmark, the Clocktower. This was on the only school in Harborne proper built by Harborne School Board; the foundation stone records its opening in 1881.*

a line from Monument Lane to Harborne, a distance of less than three miles. It was intended that the line would run to Lapal, where it would join a proposed Halesowen to Bromsgrove route, but this line was never built. The company office was in London, and there were no local directors. The project stalled. Not until 10 August 1874 was the Harborne line opened, with the LNWR operating it from Monument Lane shed. It remained an independent company until railway grouping in 1922. Two years after the Harborne Railway, the Birmingham West Suburban Railway opened a station at Somerset Road, Edgbaston, which was of use to Harborne commuters at the north-east end of the village. This was worked by the Midland Railway.

The new railways gave further impetus to house building, particularly in Station Road, Park Hill Road and Wentworth Road, at first called Wellington Road until the duplication of the name in Edgbaston caused problems. The pathway to the station from Park Hill Road is still open. These new homes were substantial, with three storeys, including servants' rooms, and were built for the growing middle class. Many individual houses were designed by A.B. Phipson; these included 26 and 28 York Street, 79 Greenfield Road, and houses in Serpentine Road. For the benefit of the new residents, a church, St John's, was built in 1856 in a newly cut road, on church land at Harborne Heath. (It was destroyed in the Second World War and the land is now occupied by houses.) Describing the church as 'handsome', the 1860 directory says it can hold 800 people. The first incumbent was Rev. Thomas Smith, who lived at the newly built Lordswood House, which ended its days as

a maternity hospital and is now replaced by Weatheroaks. His preaching was extremely controversial: a real firebrand, he attracted a congregation from as far away as Oldbury, dramatically throwing himself around in the pulpit and explaining theological points in 'a lofty style'. Traditionalists tended to avoid St John's, and indeed it seems as though the character of the two main Anglican churches in Harborne was fixed at this time. Meanwhile, the Wesleyan Methodist church on High Street had become too small and a new church was built in South Street, the foundation stones being laid in 1868. It seated 500 and cost £2,500.

The congregation of Baptists had expanded continuously since its beginning in 1787. After 1820 it had met in a private house at Harborne Heath, and later in the *Fish Inn* at the corner of North Road (Fish Lane) and Grays Road. In 1836 the congregation moved into a former Independent chapel; by 1854 their number had reached twenty-nine. In 1864 a new church was built opposite Ravenhurst Road in red-brick Gothic to replace the small chapel which had served since 1836. This earlier chapel had small iron-framed windows and its side wall was parallel to the footpath. To enter, you walked through a small garden and along a pathway. The new church bore a foundation stone of 11 October 1864. The minister at the time was Rev. Thomas McLean, a gentle and persuasive Scot, who worked in Harborne for 17 years. He was followed by the intense and cultured Rev. Alfred North. Later additions to the Baptist church were made in 1877 and again during the early years of the next century. From 1880 the Harborne church had charge of the Beech Lanes chapel, situated where

81 *Harborne Library, once the Masonic Hall.*

82 *The foundation stone of Harborne and Edgbaston Institute, now converted to housing.*

83 *The corner of Vivian Road and Greenfield Road retains the old blue enamel Birmingham street signs.*

the present car saleroom is, near the *Cock and Magpies*.

In 1870 a Mr Morris bought the old Methodist chapel in High Street, with its two adjoining cottages, and gave them to the Catholic congregation. The old building is reported to have been full of moths and swarming with bugs. It was cleaned out and there was a solemn opening ceremony on 26 June 1870. However, in 1873 the Lodge in Lodge Road (Vivian Road) came up for sale and was purchased with its land to form the site of a new church. ('Harborne Lodge'

had originally been a lodge to The Park, Theodore Price's residence.) The foundation stone was laid on 8 September 1875 and the new church was completed in 1877.

The new population set about organising sports facilities, a village institute, street lighting, protection from fires and a drainage and sewage system. Under the Forster Education Act of 1870, they were also required to set up a school board to provide enough places for every child in Harborne and Smethwick. A United Drainage Board, similar to the Poor Law Union, was set up in 1877, covering Aston, Balsall Heath, Birmingham, Handsworth, Harborne, Kings Norton, Northfield, Perry Barr and Saltley. A sewage system was certainly needed, as it was reported that previously there were open sewers down High Street. They were usually overflowing; 'we let the microbes eat one another' said a commentator.

84 *The Rev. Thomas Smith, vicar of St John's church. His congregation came from miles away to hear him preach.*

85 *Gray's Road preserves the name of Joseph Gray, one of an innkeeping family who kept at various times the* King's Head, *the* Golden Cross *and the* Plough.

86 *Yewdale, Harborne Park Road. An earlier name for this area was Tinkers Green.*

87 *A ticket from Harborne Baptist church, once situated in High Street opposite Ravenhurst Road.*

Harborne's own Local Board of Health was formed on 1 April 1864. The first meeting was in the National School in what is now Old Church Road. The dominant personality on this board was John Pix Weston, who had been a rate collector as early as 1848. By 1851 he had become Registrar of Births, Deaths and Marriages, and later Surveyor of the Highways. After the first meeting the Local Board met in

88 *The Roberts lych-gate, erected in memory of Eliza Roberts, the vicar's wife, who ran the vicarage school.*

89 *Another scene on the High Street, this time near Ravenhurst Road. The original roof of a house later faced in Victorian style can be seen on the left.*

90 *Pupils of the vicarage school in the late 1890s, outside the door of the rather grand, early 19th-century vicarage.*

91 *A late 19th-century scene in Vivian Road. Many of the buildings still stand.*

92 *The Field House in Harborne Park Road has been refurbished many times but still retains wooden beams inside. It appears in records as early as the 17th century.*

93 *A 19th-century village character: William Whitehouse of Weymoor Farm.*

Weston's house in Albert Road (now number 39). Weston was appointed Collector to the Board, being paid three per cent commission on the rates he collected. He was also secretary to the Harborne Penny Bank and the Literary Institution. He died in July 1877, by which time the Board was well established. Local Board offices were built at High Street, near Harrison's (Poyner's) farmhouse, which by this time had been turned into tenements (though the old farmhouse still sported a weathercock on its roof). The site of the new board offices had previously been an orchard. The gateway was a ceremonial stone arch, perhaps moved from another location. The proceedings of the Local Board are fully reported in the local *Harborne Herald and Smethwick News*, which ran from 1876 to 1901.

The Harborne School Board had its first meeting on 18 December 1873. The chairman was Walter Chamberlain, relative of Joseph. The board had to cover the areas of both Harborne and Smethwick, despite Smethwick now having its own Board of Health. The school board offices were in Smethwick, and in fact most of the effort and expenditure of the board went into providing schools for that town. The first school to be built was West Smethwick Board School, and this was followed by schools at Brasshouse Lane, Corbett Street and Bearwood Road (1882). Harborne itself had only one school built, York Street or High Street school, now the Clocktower Community Centre. This was opened in 1881, but it is Cape Board School at Cape Hill (1888) which still preserves the

94 *The Gardner family, including the clockmaker, William Gardner, whose skill made the Clocktower clock. The photograph is probably taken behind his shop in High Street.*

Harborne School Board name, engraved on the sculpture above the front door.

Harborne was in an anomalous position. Smethwick had far outgrown it and was developing its own institutions. Harborne proper was still a village, changing into a suburb, but with no large town population which could help to spread the rate burden. If there were to be fire cover, it would need to be on a voluntary basis: Charles Hart's sons, Charles and George, founded the fire service in 1879, opening premises in Serpentine Road after an appeal raised more than £190. By 1883 about seven fires a year were being put out. Another suburban institution was the Harborne and Edgbaston Institute. Funds were raised from the gentry and business community, and the building, including two theatres and a library, was opened in 1878. The foundation stone was laid by Shakespearian actor Henry Irving, who arrived at the nearby station in a specially chartered train. The Institute continued to produce plays and provide a meeting place for the richer citizens

until 1916. Its building is now converted to apartments. Its replacement as a library was part of the deal with Birmingham in the 1890s, when the Masonic Hall, designed by A.B. Phipson and son, was adapted for library use.

Young men's clubs were important during Victorian times. The Harborne Young Men's Bible Society was one such, but study alone was not enough. In 1868 young men's groups from the Baptist church and St Peter's formed a cricket club, which at first played just outside Harborne on fields belonging to Harrison's farm in Richmond Hill Road. In 1874 there was a move to Old Church Avenue, where the Harborne Cricket Club has played ever since. The influence appears to have been predominantly Baptist, and the St Peter's members eventually seceded, forming the Harborne Somerville Club in 1888. This team played at a ground in Queen's Park Road for many years.

A major building changed out of all recognition at this time was Harborne Hall.

95 *Old Church Avenue in the early years of the 20th century. These trees extended the vista from the rear of the church.*

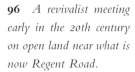

96 *A revivalist meeting early in the 20th century on open land near what is now Regent Road.*

97 *Cape Board School, Cape Hill, Smethwick. It was erected by Harborne School Board in 1888.*

Its early 19th-century alterations had left it with a Regency air (part of this still remains) but in 1885 Walter Chamberlain transformed its appearance. The new Gothic additions contrast with the classical remnants. There are stained-glass windows, arches and pinnacles, carvings and coats of arms. The exterior is terracotta red in balance with the stucco of the parts of the earlier building which remain. It would be difficult to say whether any 17th-century walls remain to remind us of Thomas Baker, the tailor. Walter Chamberlain kept exotic animals and birds in the grounds of the house, and there were stuffed deers' heads on walls and egg collections in cabinets.

As is often the case when old buildings are vanishing and old ways changing, the historians were busy. In 1885 James Kenward, businessman and poet, who had moved from Smethwick to 'Eddystone House' in Harborne, published his lectures at the Institute in the first local history book for the village, *Harborne and its Surroundings*. Its theories are fanciful, but at least it breaks new ground and shows that the history of the area was beginning to be of interest. Kenward also wrote on Welsh topics, and a poem called 'The Lay of the Old Stone' about an ice-age boulder near Smethwick old church. He was not the only poet working in Harborne at this time; Edward Capern, 'the postman poet', also produced verse, some of it featuring local scenes. Both Capern and Kenward are remembered in modern street names.

NINE

From 1887 to 1920

The 1881 census shows how far Harborne had become a Birmingham suburb, with many inhabitants born in that town. Birmingham was, by now, Chamberlain's kingdom, with municipalisation and improvement everywhere. It was not surprising that some of the chief residents of Harborne wished to become part of this enterprise, and when Birmingham put out feelers, influential people in both Harborne and Smethwick responded favourably. It seems probable that much of this support came from Birmingham-based entrepreneurs. The Harborne Local Board organised a public meeting to discuss the issue, and a motion was passed which read, '... this meeting regards with strong apprehension and disfavour the proposal to include Harborne in the extension of the ... Borough of Birmingham ... [the Borough has not] the slightest claim to annex any part of the Parish of Harborne and ... no good or useful purpose can be served thereby ...' It is notable that this was moved by Morris Baker, seconded by John Newey, and that the chairman was William Aston; all had strong roots in the neighbourhood. However, the Ratepayers' Association (dominated by the businessmen) took a different view

and called another meeting in 1889 when Birmingham's formal offer was made and debated.

Meanwhile, opposition in Smethwick grew. It became clear that the northern part of the old parish, once a hamlet, had enough resources to prosper on its own, and would soon make a bid for borough status. It is also possible that Birmingham had doubts about the inclusion of Smethwick; a Birmingham paper commented that Smethwick was 'not drained and yet has a debt of £25,000'. Attracted by the promise of a new library and a park, Harborne Local Board finally agreed to go into Birmingham in 1891, and thus the final severance between Harborne and Smethwick, and between Harborne and Staffordshire, took place. The move was crucial, since it meant that Harborne would become primarily a residential suburb, and industry would be eliminated. A hundred years later, this process was almost complete. Harborne now began to be seen as an adjunct to Edgbaston, forming part of Edgbaston ward. One of its future roles would be as an Edgbaston shopping centre. It also began to be seen as part of Warwickshire. In March 1896 there was a joint meeting of Staffordshire and Birmingham councils, and

Harborne School Board became Smethwick School Board, its Harborne school having already been transferred to Birmingham. Smethwick would remain part of Stafford-shire until it was curiously relabelled 'Warley, Worcestershire' on combining with Oldbury and Rowley Regis.

An event noted by few which took place during the discussion over Harborne's future was the birth in 1889 of a future Royal Academician, Henry Rushbury. He trained first at Birmingham School of Art (now part of the University of Central England) and became an official war artist. After retiring he was knighted, and is represented in the collection at Birmingham Art Gallery. He died in 1968 and is commemorated by a tablet in the parish church.

In 1909 Edgbaston and Harborne ward was extended to include the Halesowen parish of Quinton, the residents of which had voted by 180 to 44 to join the city. It is

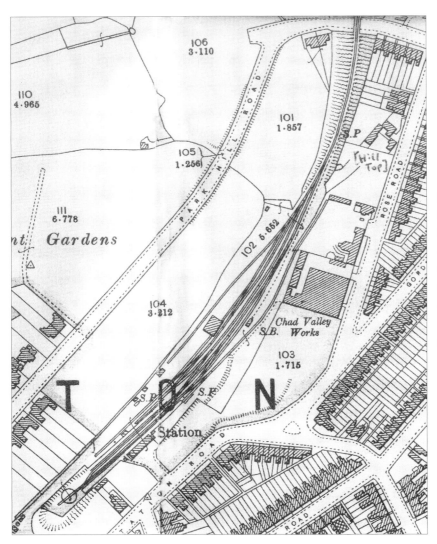

98 *Plan of Harborne railway station, showing the platform and sidings. It is thought that passenger services ceased because of a deal between the railway and Birmingham Corporation Transport Department. (OS map 1900)*

99 *A rural view across the Hilly Fields.*

not certain how much they benefited from this move, but during the next sixty years citizens from Harborne and Birmingham moved into the area so that when, during council re-organisation in the 1960s, it was proposed to add Quinton ward (including the western part of Harborne as far as Harts Green) to Warley (now Sandwell) borough, this was firmly rejected. Much of Quinton had been formerly 'the township of Ridgacre', in Shropshire with most of Halesowen. However, by 1909 Quinton included both the Worcestershire and the former Shropshire parts of the parish.

As part of Lichfield diocese, Harborne's confirmations were performed in the early years of the century by the Bishop of Lichfield, or sometimes the suffragan Bishop of Shrewsbury. But in 1905 a new diocese of Birmingham was created, with St Philip's church in Colmore Row the cathedral. In 1911 Harborne House, Thomas Green's mansion of 1781, was bought by the Church Commissioners as a residence for the bishops.

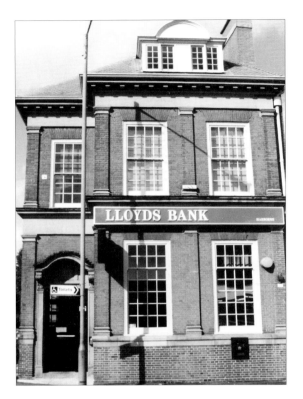

Bishop Henry Russell Wakefield was the first resident. At this time additions were made to Thomas Green's house, including a private chapel in Arts and Crafts style. Municipal facilities so long desired were now being provided. The library, located in the old masonic hall on High Street, was opened in 1892, and public subscription provided a park, Queen's Park, which opened on 5 October 1898 to celebrate Queen Victoria's Diamond Jubilee. It included 14 acres of what had been pasture land, and the watercourse running down to Harts Green from behind Earls Court Road, so could provide a pond. It was stipulated that children's play facilities should be included

100 *The elegant façade of Lloyds Bank in High Street near the Junction.*

101 *Harborne bus garage from Serpentine Road. It was opened in 1926 to serve the expanding transport needs of Harborne and Quinton and closed in 1986.*

and they are again available in 2004. In 1906 Court Oak House was purchased and added to the park. Lightwoods Park was opened in 1903 on land once owned by Sir Francis Galton. A special feature is the Shakespeare Garden, opened on 22 July 1915. This park, at the southern edge of Bearwood, was and is still technically outside Birmingham boundaries.

Municipal transport took a little longer. Although a Birmingham Corporation Tramways department was formed in 1903, it was not until 1917 that Harborne village bus routes were transferred to the city from Midland Red. These had developed from the days of 'Noah's Ark', the strange-

looking horse-bus which began its journey by the church and took one hour to reach Birmingham. Before 1917 there used to be a Sunday horse-bus service from Harborne to Bartley Green, for people to walk round Frankley. Other horse-buses ran only twice a week from Harborne to Bartley Green, via California and Jiggins Lane. These vehicles seem to have lasted until about 1920, with a fare of 6d. each way from the *Duke of York* to Bartley Green. Bus services were still less important than the train. The 1910 timetable shows more than thirty trains on a weekday from New Street to Harborne, from 7 o'clock in the morning until 11 p.m.

102   *A scene towards the top of Harborne Park Road. The road was doubled in the 1920s, at first in order to run trams down the reservation. This plan was never carried out, and buses ran the No. 11 route.*

New housing development went on apace in the early years of the new century. Terrace houses with rear extensions were built near the station in Rose Road, Gordon Road and Park Hill Road and near the bus route at Earls Court Road and Hampton Court Road, both of which were near the new Queen's Park. Victoria Road and War Lane also had terrace rows. The external design of these new houses often had classical features such as pillars and garlands; they were made of red brick with stone decoration. For the benefit of the new houses near Queen's Park, Court Oak Primitive Methodist church was opened in 1903. St Faith's Mission church was also opened in 1906 to serve the same area. Meanwhile Quinton parish had built a similar small mission church in Aubrey Road; these would combine in 1933 to become St Faith's and St Laurence's.

During this time old houses on High Street were being converted into shops selling almost everything. Opposite the *Green Man*, Thomas Carter sold bread and cakes, and on the same row were a cycle dealer and a tobacconist. Between Station Road and Albany Road were 34 shops, including Keith Pilley the draper, specialising in funeral clothes, Hedgecock, the picture frame maker, Walter Mudd's fish game and rabbit, a rival, Charles Lloyd, who sold oysters, a hairdresser, cabinet maker, tailor, stationer and boot and shoe maker. Many of these advertised in the parish magazine, which reached most of the houses in Harborne.

103 *Looking up High Street from near the Clocktower. The Harborne Stores still stands on the corner of Station Road.*

104 *The old horse trough at the Junction, High Street. Many efforts have been made to locate this since its disappearance in the 1960s, but without success.*

One of the most notable shops was W.A. Shaw, the dispensing 'chymist', whose premises on the corner of High Street and Albany Road lasted almost a century before becoming an estate agents. Shaw's shop was purpose-built and set the tone for a suburban, not a village, shopping centre. Calling himself the West City Pharmacy, Shaw is clearly stating that he intends to be metropolitan. He boasts a photographic 'depot' and sells also 'toilet and Sick Room Requisites, Natural Mineral waters and Purest Sparkling Aerated Waters'. He will exercise 'the most scrupulous care' in preparing all medicines, which he will dispense person-ally, giving the matter his 'direct attention'. Many Harborne residents throughout the 20th century had cause to be grateful. One trade which is no longer practised went on at Mrs Hunt's 'Registry Office for Servants', through which a 'large number of General Servants, Cooks, Parlourmaids, Housemaids,

Nurserymaids &c' were continually 'being suited'.

In 1904 the *Junction Inn* was rebuilt, using red brick and terracotta. Like Shaw's opposite, it was not a village building, but one intended to present urbanity. It has now become an important landmark, though currently it operates under a different name. In front of it was a horse trough, given by a local business. The disappearance of this horse trough in the latter half of the 20th century was a mystery into which local councillors have probed without success. Sir Henry Wiggin of Metchley Grange, a superb mansion near Malins Road which had served him for not much more than fifteen years, died the following year. He was a philanthropist who gave the Wiggin Cottage Homes for elderly people, and is remembered by a monument in the parish church. For some time he had performed the function of the last squire of Harborne,

105 *Harborne's memorial to the dead of two world wars. Located in the parish churchyard, this is the destination of the Armistice Day ceremony each November.*

becoming Lord Mayor of Birmingham and MP for East Staffordshire, as well as accepting such offices as president of Harborne Golf Club.

The development of modern garden cities, for example at Letchworth and, near at hand, in Bournville, had caused philanthropic manufacturers to consider the housing conditions of their workers. In Harborne, the Moor Pool estate was the idea of John Sutton Nettlefold, a member of a Unitarian family related to the Chamberlains and a screw manufacturer whose factory was in Grove Lane, Smethwick. His aim was to build a new, airy estate with a variety of houses intended to cater for a cross-section of the community. Density was nine to the acre, although legally forty to the acre would have been permissible. Fifty-four acres of land, formerly Poyner's Farm and the Hill Top Farm, was used to build 500 houses. Nettlefold determined that only high quality building materials should be used. Bricks were locally produced and Scandinavian pine was imported. Amenities included a bowling green, still in use, a hall (in which Moorpool players perform) and a green, now the tennis courts. One of the important features was the Moor Pool itself, the pool which had supplied generations of villagers with water to wash clothes and a swimming place for the village lads. Roads were all provided with grass verges, though in the age of the car the roads do seem rather narrow.

The first turf was cut by Mrs Nettlefold on 26 October 1907, and building began the following January. Though a similar design was used for all the dwellings, there was great variation in size, from small flats to larger gabled semis. These differences were reflected in the rents, which ranged from 4s. 8d. to 11s. The estate was vested in Harborne Tenants Ltd in 1907, and was complete by 1912, Carless Avenue forming the final part. Co-ownership of the estate was the first position of the founders, though since then individual tenants have been allowed to buy their properties and some have been sold on the open market.

At the other end of Harborne a further crucial development took place. George Hart and Arthur Godlee had been the prime movers in forming Harborne Golf Club, renting Home Farm from the York family at £25 per annum. The actual date of establishment was 14 October 1893. Early in 1901 the land came up for sale, and a syndicate of golf club members decided to lease it, thus ending problems over the lease of some of the fields. Prior to this, the club had been using land on the tithe barn farm

106 *The cows come home to Weymoor Farm. This was one of the last working farms in Harborne, retaining a flock of hens until the 1960s.*

107 *St Mary's Road in the early 20th century. The road was then newly cut through the fields at the side of the Field House.*

THE FREEHOLD OF THIS PARK WAS PURCHASED BY
THE PEOPLE OF HARBORNE
UNDER THE AUSPICES OF
THE HARBORNE CHARITY FETE COMMITTEE
AND PRESENTED TO THE CITY COUNCIL
IN COMMEMORATION OF
THE SIXTIETH YEAR OF THE REIGN OF
QUEEN VICTORIA.

108 *Queen's Park was paid for by public subscription and opened to celebrate Queen Victoria's Jubilee. It occupies land once part of the Birch family's demesne.*

site (now Church Farm golf course). The whole of Home Farm was up for sale and this was the last time that the well-known field names such as Dimmings Dale and Ox Leasow were used; the golf course would obliterate them. However, the Home Farm buildings still stand, and the golf course remains a large open lung for this part of Harborne, with its right of way (previously 'The Old Market Road') still in use as a footpath. The final move was to buy the whole of the golf course area in 1921 for £18,300.

Both church-run and maintained schools were expanding in this period. In 1902 Birmingham School Board opened its first and only school in Harborne in Station Road. This was built on a site originally part of Harborne Heath and was well placed to accommodate pupils from the newly devel-oping areas in St John's parish. However, St Peter's, the original National School, was also extended, the parts fronting Old Church Road being added at this time. Catholic pupils were provided with new buildings in Vivian Road, alongside the new Catholic church of St Mary's. Until then they had been taught in the old Wesleyan building on the High Street. St John's School, originally built in 1862 on the site of the present church, land which had originally been called Matchcroft and had been part of the parish land since the 17th century, lost pupils to the new council school. It was eventually closed in 1917 and a new frontage put on in 1921 when it became the memorial hall. A private boarding school was successfully run at the vicarage in the 1890s by Mrs Roberts, whose husband, Rev. Edward Roberts, died in 1891 after forty years' ministry at the

109 *The Wiggin Cottages in Margaret Road. They were endowed by Sir Henry Wiggin of Metchley Grange, whose life is commemorated by a mural tablet in the parish church.*

110 *St Peter's School has been expanded many times. New building has always reflected the original 1830s style; this is a major addition from the early years of the 20th century.*

parish church. He had been much loved by the poor, and gentle yet 'firm in the interests of the Church'. His widow was also well loved and after her death the final lych–gate, facing what is now St Peter's Road, was erected to her memory. In 1919 Harborne Hall became a boys' preparatory school, with buses running to and from Kings Heath and Moseley for day boys, although boarders were also taken. The school advertised 'electric light throughout', with a chapel and a farm (on part of the old rectory site): 37 acres in all.

111 *The Baptist church issued for a time the* Pioneer *magazine. This edition dates from 1895.*

112 *The magazine of St Peter's church records many local shops through their advertisements down the years. These examples are from about 1902.*

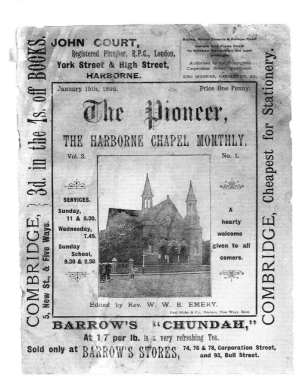

Other educational establishments which date from this time include the Tennal Industrial School, which has gone through many changes to become eventually the Martineau Education Centre, and the Blind Institute. Tennal School began in Gem Street, Birmingham, as an initiative to retrain orphans and minor delinquents, and later became a 'reformatory'. It was generally known as the 'Ansell School'. The Blind Institute was founded in 1903 as an offshoot of the Royal Institution for the Blind in Edgbaston, and erected on what had been part of the Burnt Heath. At this point it was a kindergarten, but its functions have developed and it is now the Birmingham centre for education and training for the blind, with workshops and living accommodation as part of the facilities.

The parish church had not forgotten its function as teacher. The Sunday school had many volunteer members of staff and the annual prize distribution was a matter concerning the whole of the village community. One such took place on Monday 23 September 1903, with an 'unusually good programme of recitations, songs, dialogues, etc., by the children, and addresses ... given by the clergy and superintendents'. On this occasion a second night was needed to give all the prizes to the infants, because, when the two schools were combined, the 'little tots' ended the evening with their eyes blinking. On both nights, however, the finale was to be buns and 'God bless you'. It was here in Harborne that the world's first Girl Guide troop was founded in 1909. Its official title was the 1st Harborne and the 1st Birmingham Girl Guide Company.

In 1913 appeared one of only two books on Harborne history from the early years

113 *The Moor Pool estate was much more than a housing scheme. It had its own community activities, as this advertisement from the Coronation Festival in 1911 shows.*

of local history writing. This was *Harborne Once upon a Time* by 'Tom Presterne', a pseudonym for Thomas Priest, whose father had been a spectacle maker on the corner of Ravenhurst Road and High Street. In the book Priest draws on memories from his father and grandfather, recalling episodes in Harborne from the beginning of the 19th century. It is a marvellous storehouse of local legend, interspersed with comment of an improving nature, which gives us a very clear picture of the times in which Priest lived. His eye-witness accounts of the village in the early years of the 20th century are enthralling, as are the memories he shares with a friend he calls 'Undertone'. Village characters such as Job Freeth, who had died in 1811, are faithfully described in this vivid book and tales of a very rural pre-Victorian Harborne are preserved.

In the light of Harborne's recent almost wholly residential development, it is worth noting the progress of industry at the turn of the 20th century. This is exemplified by Johnson's Chad Valley Works at the top of Rose Road. The factory, into which operations were moved from Birmingham, opened in 1897. At first the concentration was on stationery and printing, but soon the firm developed the production of games. By 1902 they were advertising Table Tennis as 'the great society game', and it could be bought in the Ethel Street branch in the city centre. Employment was given to many Harborne women in the stitching and cutting parts of the factory, while the office staff included typists and female clerks.

However, the printing remained in male hands.

By now a coal distribution trade had developed near the station, with Charles Minshull setting up an enterprise, aiming to deliver coal 'promptly at lowest prices'. His competitors were Dickin Brothers, with outlets at Harborne station and at Hagley Road Wharf, the next station towards Birmingham on the Harborne Railway. By 1903 Bruce Edmonds was added to the list of coal merchants, also working from Harborne station.

John Holt's organ factory moved to the Pioneer Works, Station Road in 1899. The firm specialised in small free-standing organs, but the trade was badly affected by the First World War and the site has been redeveloped as Clarence Mews for housing. Thomas Priest records the demise of earlier

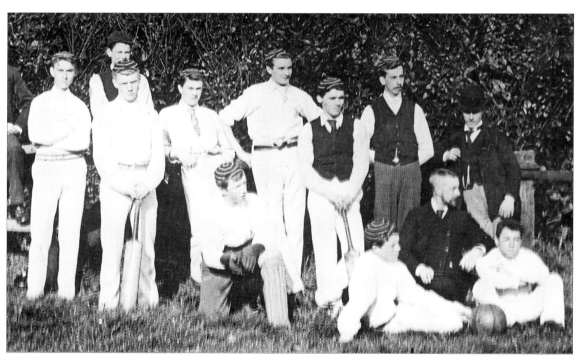

114 *Harborne Cricket Club has roots as far back as 1868. Here are some unknown players in 1903.*

LOCAL TIME TABLE—HARBORNE BRANCH.

WEEK DAYS.

	am	am	am	am	am	am	pm	pm	pm	pm	pm	pm	pm	pm	pm	pm	pm	pm	pm
BIRMINGHAM (New St.) ....dep.	7 0	7 35	9 0	10 10	11 5	12 10	12*50	12*50	...	1*15	1*15	1*25	1*50	2 8	3 0	3 25	3 58	4 17	4*50
Monument Lane	7 3	7 38	9 3	10 13	11 8	12 13	...	12*54	1*3	1*18	1*18	1*29	1*53	2 13	3 3	3 29	4 1	4 21	4*53
Icknield Port Road	7 6	7 41	...	...	...	12 16	...	12*57	1*6	1*21	1*21	1*32	1*56	2 15	...	3 32	...	4 24	4*56
Rotton Park Road	7 9	7 44	9 10	10 17	11 12	12 21	12*58	1*0	1*9	...	1*24	1*35	1*59	2 20	3 7	3 36	4 6	4 28	4*59
Hagley Road	7 12	7 47	9 18	10 20	11 15	12 23	1*1	1 3	1*11	1*24	1*27	1*38	2 3	3 2	3 10	3 39	4 9	4 31	5* 2
HARBORNE .... arrive	7 16	7 52	9 22	10 24	11 19	12 26	1* 3	1 7	1*14	1*28	1*31	1*42	2 7	2 27	3 14	3 43	4 13	4 35	5* 6

WEEK DAYS—continued.

	pm	pm	pm	pm	pm	pm	pm	pm	pm	pm	pm	pm	pm	pm
BIRMINGHAM (New St.) ....dep.	5 15	5*35	6 0	6*15	6 40	7* 0	7 20	7*40	8 15	8*50	9 20	10 0	10 40	11 15
Monument Lane	5 18	5*38	...	6*19	6 43	7* 4	7 24	7*44	8 18	...	9 23	10 3	...	11 4 11 19
Icknield Port Road	5 21	5*41	...	6*22	6 46	7* 6	7 26	7*47	8 21	...	9 26	10 6	10 45	11 7 11 22
Rotton Park Road	5 24	5*44	6 6	6*25	6 50	7* 9	7 29	7*50	8 24	8*56	9 29	10 9	10 48	11 11 11 25
Hagley Road	5 28	5*47	6 10	6*28	6 53	7*12	7 33	7*54	8 27	8*59	9 32	10 12	10 51	11 14 11 28
HARBORNE .... arrive	5 32	5*51	6 13	6*32	6 57	7*16	7 37	7*57	8 31	9* 3	9 36	10 16	10 55	11 18 11 32

WEEK DAYS.

	am	am	am	am	am	am	am	am	am	am	am	am	am	pm	pm	pm	pm
HARBORNE ....dep.	5 35	6 35	7 25	7 39	7 8	8 24	8 36	8 53	9 8	9 33	10 5	10 42	11 30	12 35	1*50	1*55	2* 3
Hagley Road	5 37	6 37	7 27	7 41	8 9	8 26	8 38	8 55	9 10	9 35	10 7	10 44	11 32	12 37	1*52	1*57	2* 5
Rotton Park Road	5 40	6 40	7 30	7 45	8 12	8 29	8 41	8 58	9 14	9 38	10 10	10 47	11 35	12 40	1*55	2* 0	2* 8
Icknield Port Road	5 42	6 42	7 32	7 48	8 14	8 31	8 45	9 0	9 16	9 40	...	10 49	...	12 42	1*57	2* 3	2*10
Monument Lane	5 45	6 45	7 35	7 51	8 17	8 34	...	9 3	9 19	9 43	10 15	10 53	11 39	12 46	2* 0	2* 6	2*13
BIRMINGHAM (New St.) ... arrive	5 51	6 51	7 41	7 57	8 23	8 40	8 52	9 9	9 25	9 50	10 20	10 58	11 45	12 51	2* 6	2*12	...

WEEK DAYS—continued.

	pm	pm	pm	pm	pm	pm	pm	pm	pm	pm	pm	pm	pm	pm
HARBORNE ....dep.	2*13	2 47	3 30	4 1	4 23	4 42	5 20	6 0	6 45	7*25	8 6	8 40	9 45	10 25 11 5
Hagley Road	2*15	2 49	3 32	4 3	4 25	4 44	5 22	6 2	6 47	7*27	8 8	8 42	9 47	10 27 11 7
Rotton Park Road	2*19	2 52	3 36	4 6	4 29	4 47	5 26	7 6	6 51	7*30	8 11	8 45	9 50	10 30 11 11
Icknield Port Road	...	2 54	...	4 8	...	4 49	5 29	6 9	6 53	7*32	8 13	8 47	9 52	10 32 11 13
Monument Lane	2*24	2 57	3 40	4 12	4 34	4 52	5 32	6 15	6 56	7*35	8 16	8 50	9 55	10 35 11 16
BIRMINGHAM (New St.) .. arrive	2*29	3 3	3 46	4 17	4 39	4 58	5 37	6 20	7 2	7*41	8 22	8 56	10 1	10 41 11 22

* Saturdays excepted   ‡ Saturdays only.

115   *The Harborne train timetable for 1911.*

industrial ventures: his own father's spectacle making at the top of Ravenhurst Road, John Palmer's hammers and wrenches near the top of Balden Road, Noah Smallwood's gun implements at Metchley Lane, and Millington's steel conversion at Harborne Mill. Many Harborne workers travelled to factories in Birmingham, including the jewellery quarter. From the south of the parish, some men walked to work in Smart's brick works at California. This works had its own clay pit; in 1907 men worked a 12-hour day, from 6 a.m. to 6 p.m., digging clay and stoking fires, while women were the moulders, forcing clay through the rectangular apertures which turned them into long strips from which bricks were cut. This brickyard was on a historic site between Weoley Castle and Stonehouse. There was also another brick works, more local still, on land at the foot of Harborne Park Road, now vanished into Harborne Lane's northern extension.

The First World War had little direct effect on Harborne. Nowhere in Harborne was deliberately targeted, though there were local raids on Halesowen. Harborne Hall was first used as a home for Belgian refugees, under the supervision of a group of exiled nuns from Antwerp. Later, the Hall became an auxiliary hospital for the large numbers of wounded soldiers being sent back from France. Several temporary buildings were erected in the grounds and there was a large wooden dining hall. Convalescent patients helped to look after the pigs and grow vegetables. Much of the impetus for this came from the firm of W. & T. Avery, and the Harborne hospital became known in many parts of the world as the 'Avery Hospital'.

TEN

The 1920s to the Second World War

After the First World War Harborne settled into its new role as one of the premier suburbs of a rapidly expanding City of Birmingham while retaining a village character. Though at this point it was not clear that eventually almost all industry would be removed from what was now known as Harborne ward, it was soon the case that most Harborne residents were employed beyond the boundaries, in Birmingham offices and factories, or in the growing complexes at Selly Oak or Longbridge. After 1926 the bus link with Bournville induced an increasing number of residents to work for Cadbury's. Transport had quickly become an issue. All other areas of Birmingham had cheap transport by tram to the city centre. No trams entered Harborne, except for the No. 34 Hagley Road route at Bearwood (No. 29 via Cape Hill and Dudley Road stopped at the end of Bearwood Road).

In July 1924 new top-covered buses were introduced on the No. 3 and 4 routes from Birmingham to Queen's Park and Harborne village respectively. These initially ran from Tennant Street Garage behind Broad Street, but it was clear that further expansion in Harborne and Quinton would require a purpose-built garage. The site chosen was the Neweys' old timber yard behind the Georgian terrace near the *Duke of York*. An imposing stone-capped frontage looked out on Serpentine Road, but most buses entered and left by the back entrance in Lonsdale Road. An important decision had to be taken in 1926, when a Birmingham Outer Circle route was planned. This involved cutting a new carriageway to the west of the existing Harborne Park Road and widening Lordswood Road. At the start it had seemed that trams from Selly Oak garage could run this route, but passenger reaction to the Hagley Road routes, where buses were now competing with the trams, showed a clear preference for buses, which could pull in to the kerb and did not need expensive track or overhead wires, which were unsightly. The Outer Circle would be a bus route, partly run from Harborne garage.

These new developments meant that time was called both on the No. 34 tram and the railway route from Harborne to the city. In 1922 there were still twenty trains a day between Harborne and Birmingham New Street, but traffic declined dramatically after this. Not for much longer would the 'Harbornite' pupils travelling to King Edward's School in New Street dominate the

116 *Welsh House brook near its confluence with the unnamed brook from Tibbets Lane on Harborne Municipal Golf Course.*

Harborne line. Meanwhile other carriage-way improvements were taking place, when Northfield Road was widened near Home Farm, in 1924, for example. In 1934 a new fleet of Daimler buses with integrated staircases began work on the Harborne and Quinton routes. With the transport infrastructure in place, it became possible for small houses to be built along the No. 3 and 12 bus routes, on the site of large mansions (Oaklands Avenue, Fellows Lane, Stapylton Avenue) and on old farmland such as Weymoor and Harts Green (the farm-house was demolished in 1934); many of these did not need garages and sold for between six and seven hundred pounds.

Larger houses with garages were built in the 1930s on agricultural land in Knightlow Road and Croftdown Road. Individual houses built to customer specification began to fill Oakham Road and others. These new houses in the north of Harborne needed no public transport until wartime petrol rationing necessitated the introduction of the No. 10 bus route. The residential area at Moor Pool estate, within easy reach of Harborne station, was left without either bus route or garages for cars when passenger services from Harborne station were withdrawn in November 1934. (It is said that this was effected through a secret deal between the LMS Railway and Birmingham City

Transport.) Older Victorian houses attracted some distinguished residents, among whom was the poet W.H. Auden, now commemorated by a blue plaque at the front of Harborne baths.

Birmingham City Council had been early in the field of council housing, and was now seeking to rehouse people from delapidated housing in the city centre. Tennal Hall estate, near the terminus of the No. 3 bus, was bought and new council houses were built there, in Tennal Road, West Boulevard and other adjacent roads, both on the Harborne side of the boundary and in what had been Warley Wigorn. Remnants of Pitts Wood can still be seen here, the name probably deriving from the local sand pits prevalent in the area. Woodhouse Road is named after the fields once called Woodhouse Lands. Tennal Hall itself, the scene of Job Freeth's

struggle with poor law administration and perhaps of the Milwards' entertainment of Queen Elizabeth I, was demolished. There were protests, and as a concession to amenity the houses on the actual site were built back from the road, and a small children's play area was left by the brook south of the houses. Soon more council houses were built on the Quinton side of the boundary (the Edgbaston Golf Course site), and Harborne became physically joined to Quinton. When the golf course was built on, the club house became the site of 'Quinborne' library and community centre, which has catered for the need for meeting rooms over a wide area round Ridgacre since. Harborne ward in the 1930s stretched from the old Harborne boundary at the *Green Man* to the far end of Quinton village, near the Methodist church.

117 *The new church at Court Oak. St Faith's was begun before the 1939 war, but not completed until the 1950s.*

118 *Before 1947 there was no secondary school within Harborne. These children from Station Road won places at secondary schools elsewhere in 1935. They are, from left to right, back to front: Roy Morrell, Barbara Price, John Morgan, Raymond Wright, Cynthia Tracy, Kenneth Tasker; Dorothy Jones, Betty Reynolds, Irene Minchin, Brenda Lea, Doreen Mogg, Peggy Plimley; Roy Margets, Marie Evans, Violet French, Neville Jones.*

A parallel step towards providing council housing was the purchase by the city council in 1932 of most of the land of Weymoor Farm. Development here was interrupted by the war and the farmhouse was not demolished until 1965. During its final 30 years the venerable house, with its flocks of hens, remained a rural landmark; indeed, during the war hens became vital to the area's economy, and many smaller houses had hen coops in the back garden. In plan, Weymoor was similar to the *Bell*, having a long main house, with two projecting wings, each gabled.

For entertainment, the better off now climbed into their cars and went to town, to attend the Repertory Theatre or Theatre Royal, the Midland Institute or town hall concerts given by the City of Birmingham orchestra, or to take genteel tea at Barrows. Live theatre was also represented by the Windsor in Bearwood, popular at panto-mime season. In Harborne, this was the age of building or rebuilding public houses, entertainment for the less well-off. Near the top of Harborne Hill the old *Green Man* was demolished in 1938-9 and a large roadhouse erected, maintaining the name. The *King's*

119   *Chad Valley Toys was Harborne's major industry between the wars. Here are the Chad Valley staff in 1928.*

Arms was refaced with mock-Tudor beams like those on people's houses. A new public house replaced the *Woodman* at Queen's Park: the very splendid *Court Oak*, with its three-dimensional pub sign giving a new meaning to the idea of 'court', preserved a name from the dawn of Harborne history. At the far south, the old *Golden Cross* was demolished and a new building substituted. Of the early pubs only the *New Inn*, the *Bell* and the *Plough* remained in their original premises, two of them reminders of the enterprise of the Gray family, while the *Bell* kept its 17th- and 18th-century rooms intact and stood witness to the Luckocks and Stevenses. The *Duke of York* and *King's Head* had been rebuilt much earlier and,

across the Hagley Road, on the edge of Lightwoods Park, the *Old Talbot* was now called the *Dog*. Many of these were Mitchells and Butlers pubs, their beer supplied in horse-drawn drays, with fine teams of black horses to pull them.

Harborne Golf Club was now well established on the fields which had been Home Farm, the farm so neatly inventoried on the death of Robert Rotton. Influential members such as E. Grice and J.P. Richards were Harborne residents, but the club was increasingly attracting members from further afield. In 1928 the course was extended though the purchase of 58 acres of Welsh House Farm. Harborne Cricket Club reached its 70th anniversary in 1938, and the

120 *Harborne's Territorial Army barracks in Court Oak Road. It was here that the Bomb Disposal unit worked in the Second World War. Onneley House now occupies the site.*

hockey club also prospered, playing regularly in local competitions. The Municipal Golf Course (Church Farm) opened in 1924, providing subsidised golf for the growing population over fields which had been part of Tithe Barn Farm. A small part of this land, part of Rectory Farm, which had been originally sold in 1856 by Howard Simcox, was retained as the verger's house and garden. Public swimming baths were opened in Lordswood Road on 13 December 1928. During the 1930s the cinema became a major form of popular entertainment. First on the scene in Harborne was the Picture House, Serpentine Road, and this was followed by the Royalty, now the bingo hall. Just as war loomed a sumptuous new

building was opened on the Oldbury side of Hagley Road West, just across the border at Beech Lanes, the Warley Odeon.

Residential expansion, especially of council houses in the area where Harborne now merged into Quinton, meant that new school provision was needed. Plans were made for a new school at Woodhouse Road, and for an enlargement of St Peter's Church School. Land near the verger's cottage behind the churchyard was earmarked for this, but (luckily for the preservation of the oldest school buildings in Birmingham) the war interrupted. Billy Hardwick, the headmaster, had already begun collecting material relating to Harborne history, and we still owe him a debt of gratitude for the collections of

121 *Harborne swimming baths, opened in 1928.*

newspaper cuttings and photographs which he left to posterity in the local libraries. In the centre of Harborne children divided their school life between the original school board building at York Street, now called High Street, and the newer site at Station Road, enlarged in 1928. After 1931 infants' and senior sections were at Station Road, the buildings of which were enhanced by the addition of temporary classrooms for cookery classes, while the juniors attended High Street. Playground games preserved typical south Staffordshire terminology: tag was 'tick', and the seeker was 'on', while to call a truce one crossed fingers and shouted 'barley'. Roman Catholic children attended St Mary's School in Vivian Road, where an annual summer fête saw the production of Milton's *Comus* in 1926. The school was enlarged in 1937.

A number of small private schools catered for the more aspiring. Among these were Harborne Collegiate School at Court Oak Road, following the closure in 1924 of Harborne Preparatory School at Harborne Hall. However, many more prosperous Harborne parents sent their children to private schools in Edgbaston. There were no grammar schools in Harborne, and those who passed what is now known as the 11-plus would go to Five Ways or George Dixon's in Edgbaston, or to Kings Norton schools. In 1930 the Birmingham Bluecoat School moved from the city centre to a site opposite the *Green Man* on part of what was once Harborne Heath. One of the architects was a Harborne man, Mr H.W. Simister.

Increasing population also had an effect on the health provision for the area. The best-known Harborne medical practice was that set up by Dr Lucas Middleton in York Street in 1880. After five years he built a house for himself with a surgery attached in Albany Road; this house still exists. In 1922 it was bought by Dr Hugh Morton, who used it as his home and surgery until his death in 1969. Dr Morton was very well known throughout Harborne, and sadly missed. The Harborne Society decided to replant part of the front garden of the Clocktower and erect a memorial plaque to him in 1980, thus commemorating both Dr Morton and the opening of the first doctor's surgery in 1880. By now the practice had moved to premises in Albert Road, while its next-door neighbour, previously No. 8 Albert Road and the surgery of the other Harborne doctors, moved its facilities to Lordswood Medical Centre.

On the southern edge of Harborne, in Metchley Park, it was decided to build a new hospital for the region, to which some facilities would transfer from the centre of Birmingham. This was the 'Queen Elizabeth', built partly on land once occupied by the Roman camp. Private roads were built from the *Golden Cross* and the Edgbaston side to take hospital traffic. It is extraordinary that, as late as 1937, the growth in car use was unforeseen, so that these roads are now choked. The hospital was not served by public transport until the extension of the 2B service from the *Ivy Bush* in 1939, which skirted Harborne, leaving Harborne Lane at the *Golden Cross*.

The western growth of Harborne on the boundary with Quinton necessitated a re-examination of Church of England

122 *The opening of the Queen Elizabeth Hospital. This is the scene near the* Golden Cross *in 1938.*

provision there. As long ago as 1904 a small mission hall of corrugated iron had been erected near Queen's Park and dedicated to St Faith. There was another small temporary building just in Quinton parish at Redhall Road, Beech Lanes, dedicated to St Laurence. In October 1933 the two church congregations joined together to become St Faith's and St Laurence's, and it was determined that a new church would be built, to be designed by local architect Philip Chatwin. The foundation stone was laid in May 1936, but after the church had been dedicated the Second World War intervened, and it was not completed until 1960. The bells were brought from the redundant church of All Saints, Hockley, and the organ case incorporates wood from the pews of the closed St Michael's church, Smethwick.

Despite the dominance of housing for Birmingham, Harborne remained an industrial suburb during the 1920s and '30s. Toys, wood-framed sheds, organs, printing, and dairy products were typical of the output, and laundries still flourished. A major transport industry was centred on the station and bus garage. The most important employer

123 *The Hilly Fields before the Second World War, looking towards the brook confluence and the hill up to the church.*

124 *Harborne St Peter's Young People's Drama Society in 1931.*

125 *Buses parked in Harborne Park Road after the Second World War. Dispersal was originally to avoid enemy action, but continued because of shortage of space.*

was Chad Valley Toys. Their factory, which had been expanded by Johnson Brothers in the 1920s, was situated at the end of Rose Road. Premises at Harborne Institute had long been used for their printing, while various kinds of toys were made at Rose Road. A principal product in the 1930s was jigsaws, and soft toy making was transferred to Wellington, Shropshire. The Mirror Laundry occupied the Weekin Works at Park Hill Road (showing that washerwomen were still to be found in Harborne), but this too would later become part of the Chad Valley empire.

126 *St Peter's football team before the Second World War.*

127 *A view inside the parish church taken between 1934 and 1947.*

John Holt, Piano and Organ Manufacturers, which had moved from the centre of Birmingham at the turn of the century, continued for some time to specialise in small organs, but these became less and less popular as the century went on. Though repairs enabled the firm to continue through the war, it closed shortly afterwards. Wooden sheds were made and assembled at Phipps' in the High Street, while Follows' dairy took over part of the old mill buildings near the *Golden Cross*. There were a number of small boot and shoe repairers in the High Street and side streets, and repairing and servicing cars became a new industry, with All Electric garage at Queen's Park and Tonks' near the *Green Man* dominating. The coal distribution trade continued, as exemplified by Thomas Otley in Harborne Park Road.

Much of this steady change was interrupted at the outbreak of the Second World War. Air-raid wardens had headquarters in Queen's Park and the army barracks at the corner of Wood Lane became a bomb disposal unit. A branch of the Home Guard was formed. Barrage balloons were stationed on the cricket ground, as well as in neighbouring Warley Woods and at Bartley Green. Blackout regulations were introduced and vehicles were fitted with shades over headlights. After disastrous air raids on Hockley and Highgate Road garages in November 1940, Birmingham City Transport decided that buses must be dispersed, and those from Harborne garage were parked overnight in rows in Lonsdale Road and Harborne Park Road, while a further fuel-saving measure meant that some buses remained parked in the city centre after the morning rush hour until the afternoon.

The Harborne Railway was now used largely for coal deliveries, a morning train arriving before 7 a.m. The engine turntable at Harborne station was still in use at this time; it was finally removed in 1949. Because of the problems caused by buses being bombed,

128   *One of the row of large Victorian houses in Lordswood Road was home of the young W.H. Auden, poet.*

two readers of the *Railway Magazine* in 1943 wrote to suggest that passenger services should be resumed. However, the difficulties caused in joining the Stour Valley line at the junction in Ladywood could not be overcome. When it arrived by rail, coal was still moved from the station by horse and cart. Chad Valley turned over to the war effort in line with factories in other parts of Birmingham. War damage in Harborne, however, was comparatively light, with many incendiary bombs failing to cause major fires and jettisoned high explosive bombs

129 *A scene at Princes Corner, opposite the* Duke of York. *At one time this was to have become 'Harborne Square'.*

remaining unexploded. Two incendiaries which did score hits were recalled later by a Lord Mayor of Birmingham, Councillor Peter Hollingworth, whose family lived in Wentworth Road during the war. He spent part of one night dashing up and down the stairs carrying water to his father who was trying to put out a bomb in the toilet, while another burnt in the bedroom.

The present writer was evacuated with the family from a house in Yew Croft Ave-nue when two unexploded bombs landed in the garden, one on each side of the house itself. An interesting sight for small boys was provided at the barracks in Wood Lane by defused bombs which had been dug up in Harborne and elsewhere. A major loss was St John's church, wrecked in 1941. After this services were held in the war memorial hall, which had been St John's School, and which later provided the site for the present church. Warnings against air

130 *A procession for a fête near the Royalty cinema, at the junction of High Street and Greenfield Road. The Royalty still exists as a bingo hall.*

131 *St Paul's mission room became the church hall for St Peter's. Here St Peter's players are performing in the inter-war years.*

132 *The* Court Oak *public house is the successor to the* Woodman *of the 19th century. Sculpture over the entrance represents an oak, while in the car park is a statue representing an interpretation of the name.*

raids were provided by sirens mounted on public buildings, such as Harborne baths. Whenever these were heard people were to take cover in private air-raid shelters, or in the case of schoolchildren in brick-built shelters above ground in the playgrounds at High Street, Station Road, St Mary's and St Peter's. A large water tank appeared opposite the Baptist church in High Street, presumably to provide a ready source of water to extinguish incendiaries.

The need for temporary housing caused prefabs to be built in Queen's Park, on the Hagley Road, and on the Edgbaston side of Metchley Lane. The halt in development led to the retention of 19th-century cottages in North Road, Nursery Road, and at Beech Lanes and along the High Street; these would have followed 'slum' properties at Camomile Green and Gravel Bank into earlier oblivion if it had not been for the war. When Hitler's demise was finally announced, many of the population turned out in the evening to parade down High Street with lights, in a ceremonial farewell to blackout.

ELEVEN

From the Second World War to the Present Day

For a time after the war, little changed. Coal was still being delivered on horse-drawn carts from the station, buses retained their top camouflage; shops sold drearily packaged goods on ration. In the freezing early days of 1947, ice hardened on the roads and one could walk along the canals. It was soon decided to close all tram routes in Birmingham, substituting buses. In 1949 extra Outer Circle buses were transferred to Harborne, and in 1952 the Bristol Road trams were replaced by buses; in anticipation the Weoley Castle routes had been transferred to Harborne the previous year. This was balanced by the transfer of services 3, 9, 10 and 34 to the new Quinton garage, which opened in October 1949. However, both Harborne and Quinton garages later succumbed, after the deregulation of buses and privatisation. Harborne closed in 1986.

Opposite the bus garage during the post-war period was the headquarters of Stanley N. Evans' sand and gravel business. Evans successfully combined running his business with a political career as the MP for neighbouring Wednesbury. He gained notoriety as 'Featherbed Evans' after alleging that farmers in England were given featherbed treatment compared with other businesses. His sand quarry was near the old Tom Knocker's Wood, West Boulevard, and older readers will recall his dark green lorries laden with deep red sand slowly turning out of Serpentine Road into the High Street. (No one knows who 'Tom Knocker' was, and his wood has now vanished. He is supposed to have hanged himself from a tree.)

By now city planners had zoned almost all of Harborne as residential, and this meant a rise in land values for the area, and a decline in industry. However, Chad Valley actually expanded in the 1950s, taking over the old Mirror Laundry in Park Hill Road, and continuing their use of the Institute in Station Road. New council estates were developed, most prominently the Hilly Fields estate in Grove Lane, Quinton Road and district, and Cross Farm. It was thought vital to include shopping facilities, and a row of shops was built in Grove Lane. New road names sometimes reflected earlier local names. For example, Leahurst Crescent refers to The Lea, a Victorian mansion. Unfortunately, at times it seems as though names were merely filched from old maps without reference to their locations; a road called Gravel Bank is far away from the actual Gravel Bank, thus negating the old

133 *Cheyne Walk, off Greenfield Road. The name is a rather ironic acquisition from London; the walk is on the line of an ancient right of way across fields.*

local saying that if the wind were blowing from Gravel Bank it was going to rain. A further large new estate was built on the land of Welsh House Farm, served by the original farm track, now called Welsh House Farm Road. This estate included multi-storey flats, which with the flats at West Boulevard (Selcroft) provided a new and very distinctive landmark. Private developments were at Metchley Lane, Camomile Green and, much later, Tennal Lane.

The 1947 Education Act forced councils to examine their secondary provision and, as a result, first Harborne Hill school was built just inside Edgbaston and, later, boys' and girls' schools were built on open land near the *King's Head*: the two Lordswood Schools, of which the boys' was designated a technical school, since the system was to be tripartite, with grammar, technical and modern categories. Before Harborne Hill was built, non-grammar children had been returned

134 *Harborne Church and Vicarage in 1956. The Vicarage was soon to be demolished and a new vicarage and church hall built on the site. Part of the vicarage garden remained and has recently been revitalised.*

135 *The sweet and tobacco shop at the corner of Serpentine Road. This was on the ground floor of John Newey's 1797 residence.*

136 *Seats at the top of War Lane in the 1960s. At the time these made a pleasant resting place away from the traffic roar.*

to the tiny campus at Station Road after the age of eleven. When Welsh House Farm was developed, a new school was built here for primary children. Smaller independent schools such as those on Court Oak Road closed in response to pressure for housing land and improved local authority education. Nowadays the headquarters of the Open University in the West Midlands are located on a site nearly opposite North Road. Most evenings and Saturdays see hosts of students from all over the region making their way here, to a well appointed, if architecturally null, centre of higher learning.

137 *A group of parents outside St Peter's School in 1953. By this time, the school was only one option for the education of Harborne children.*

The old mansions of the rich businessmen gradually became prey to developers anxious to build as many houses as possible on small sites. The council itself used Metchley Grange, Henry Wiggin's old house, to erect tower blocks. Theodore Price's The Park, Clent House (1955), Wellington Lodge (1968), and, amazingly, The Grove (1963) were some of the casualties. In the last case, the parkland was given to the city by the Kendricks. A proposal to build council houses on it was finally defeated, but the house was demolished, part of its panelled interior being taken to the Victoria and Albert Museum in London to become 'The Harborne Room'. It appeared possible that Court Oak House and Greenfield House might share their fate, but public opinion, led by the Harborne Society, intervened. A further possible demolition was the difficult case of Lightwoods House which, being owned by Birmingham, but within the boundaries of Smethwick, was an inevitable

bone of contention. Eventually the historic building was saved on the intervention of John Hardman, stained glass manufacturers, whose beautiful premises match their craft. Exceptions to the disastrous waste of expensive architecture were Harborne House (Bishop's Croft), where land was released at the edge of the territory for housing and diocesan offices, Harborne Hall, which moved from being a convent to a multi-faith centre, then the headquarters of VSO, and Elmley Lodge, a listed mansion house in 18th-century style, though built about 1845. This was converted to flats.

A late casualty among 19th-century mansions was Stapylton House, opposite the churchyard. This had been erected in the 1840s for the curate Rev. Stapylton Bree, but by 1851 it was occupied by Edward Law, one of J.T. Law's family from Lichfield. It was demolished in 1966 and Stapylton Court flats were built on it, though the garden had been sold before the war for the building of Stapylton Avenue. However, the coach house survives as a private house and there is a wall and gate posts in St Peter's Road which were once part of the curtilage of the house; a further gate post survives in Old Church Road. A rambling red-brick building, the house overtopped the two small cottages fronting Old Church Road.

Many post-war changes seemed to threaten the character of Harborne as a pleasant residential suburb with the appearance of a village. The response came in 1960 from the Harborne Society, founded on 4 May, whose aims were to encourage commmunity spirit, promote interest in the character and history of Harborne, and represent the interests of the area by encouraging suitable conservation, opposing unsuitable developments and putting forward suggestions for the future of Harborne to the local authority. A prime mover was Miss Madeline Aston, whose father had been the chairman of the Harborne Local Board. Charles Parker, the writer whose radio ballads made such an impression on BBC listeners, was another. Over the years Eric and Mary Abbott played an untiring part in leading the society. Often it has been hard to influence authority and business, but there have been some major successes. The society is well known, but this sometimes brings problems when it is expected to 'do something' about a matter which is wholly beyond its control.

138 *Harborne Young Farmers in 1953. The club used the Glebe Field (earlier known as Flagmore) but later transferred to land near Leahurst Crescent.*

139 *Bell ringers in 1953. The church bells are still rung on Sunday evenings and for the New Year as well as at weddings and on other important occasions.*

140 *Harborne brownie pack in 1953.*

141   *Harborne bus garage with its fleet of Guy Arab 'standards'. A more modern 'Fleetline' can be seen behind No. 3015.*

142   *Memorial to Sir Henry Wiggin of Metchley Grange. He had been a benefactor and figurehead for Harborne and beyond.*

IN
LOVING MEMORY
OF
SIR HENRY WIGGIN BARONET
OF METCHLEY GRANGE IN THIS PARISH
FOR NEARLY 50 YEARS A CONSTANT
WORSHIPPER IN THIS CHVRCH WHO DIED
NOVEMBER 12TH 1905 IN HIS 82ND YEAR

HE REPRESENTED THE EASTERN DIVISION OF
STAFFORDSHIRE IN PARLIAMENT FROM 1880 TO 1885
AND THE HANDSWORTH DIVISION FROM 1885 TO 1892
HE WAS DEPVTY LIEVTENANT AND MAGISTRATE
FOR THE ABOVE COVNTY MAGISTRATE FOR
WORCESTERSHIRE AND BIRMINGHAM OF
WHICH CITY HE WAS MAYOR 1864-5

THIS TABLET IS ERECTED BY HIS WIDOW AND
CHILDREN IN TOKEN OF THE LOVE THEY BORE HIM

"WELL DONE GOOD AND FAITHFVL SERVANT
ENTER THOV INTO THE JOY OF THY LORD"

ALSO HIS WIFE
MARY ELIZABETH
WHO DIED FEBRVARY 24TH 1911
IN HER 79TH YEAR

"NOT WEIGHING OVR MERITS, BVT PARDONING OVR
OFFENCES, THROVGH JESVS CHRIST OVR LORD"

Much land in the northern part of Harborne had been owned for many years by Calthorpe Estate. During the war Beech Lanes Farm had been used as a radio station, and afterwards this part of the area became a riding school. However, in the early 1960s Calthorpe produced a new plan for Edgbaston and the parts of Harborne they owned. A glossy brochure proclaimed that Beech Lanes would absorb hundreds of families but preserve acres of open green. The centre of Beech Lanes estate is the broad sweep of Lake Meadow

143 *At the Sandwell vintage vehicle rally, preserved Quinton garage veteran No. 2548 exhibits the destination 'Bartley Green via Harborne'. The route is now Nos. 22 and 23. (Supplied by the then 2548 group)*

144 *Remembrance Day at St John's church in 1972.*

(generally called simply 'the green'). Houses are successfully mixed, more traditional styles blending with patio houses and flats. The design was by John H.D. Madin and Partners, builders of the Birmingham City Library.

It has to be admitted that not all developments in the post–war years seem to have been of benefit. For example, Queen's Park moved from being a well maintained, beautiful open area, with some useful facilities, to rather a barren, windswept site. Since 1960 the park has lost its sensory garden for the blind, its rain shelter, part of the tennis courts, a putting green, the bandstand and the pond. Despite this, the minimal children's play area is well used, and there is a clear need for this park, one of only two in Harborne proper.

A major addition to the shopping profile of the High Street came in 1965, when Victorian houses on the north side were demolished for the new 'Parade'. One of these had been for a long time the home and surgery of Dr McCook. The new shopping row had no official nameboard, and its usual name appears to be unofficial. On the other side of the High Street, near the *Green Man*, George Fisher and Co., estate agents, refurbished very successfully a row of early Victorian houses, putting in bow windows and cleaning the brickwork. This part of the High Street has been further enhanced, after the demolition of the Salvation Army Citadel, by the opening of Marks and Spencer's food store.

145 *The former Lake Meadow, at Beech Lanes, is now generally called just 'The Green'. The mini-hills were created when Calthorpe Estate landscaped the area.*

On the other side of the High Street, at the Harborne Heath end, Vickers confectioners had a bakery, which they extended in 1952 when Harborne's earliest row of cottages was demolished to provide more space. This firm was taken over by Hughleys in the 1960s and the bakery finally shut down. A row of red-brick offices was built on the site of the cottages; although these did not replicate the style of the earlier buildings, they were quite acceptable in scale and general appearance. This is now a busy junction, traffic lights having been installed to avoid widening Nursery Road. Locally known as Nursery Hill, it is an attractive street with cottage premises on the Edgbaston side from the very early 19th century, and on the Harborne side from 1851. The green area at the foot of the hill results from demolition of 1850s houses in this and North Road. The site was originally to be used for road widening.

146 *A scene at the lower end of the High Street, with the Clocktower and former shops, including Ebenezer Buildings.*

Harborne High Street ended the 20th century with a total of 156 'units'. Of these, in 1998, 22 were vacant, 72 were service outlets, and only 59 retail. Very few had local owners or occupiers: the High Street has become much like any other High Street from Kent to Yorkshire. A major reason appears to be the very high rents charged (£35,000 for a small unit). The Harborne Society has made many efforts over the years to discover who the landlords are, with partial success. On the whole, however, it seems that a process of exploitation by outsiders, begun in the mid-19th century, has continued to develop, and there seems little our modern system can do about it. There are still a few local businesses to be found, in side streets like Lonsdale Road, Vivian Road and Station Road; even in the High Street, local businesses are not extinct. Harborne traders' associations have waxed and waned, but are not always supported by the multiples.

For many years the parish church of St Peter's used St Paul's room in Harborne Park Road as its church hall. Though this was nearer to the village centre it was not convenient for congregational use after church. A new hall was built adjoining the churchyard, Mrs Neville Chamberlain laying the foundation stone on 3 October 1953. This is now the Infants' School hall. Remarkably, within ten years the situation changed, and a more ambitious programme of expansion was begun. A new hall, vicarage, curate's house and verger's house were built, ensuring the demolition of the old verger's house, which had stood near the churchyard for two hundred years. The foundation stone of the new hall was laid by the veteran churchman, Walter Pickard, who, in many capacities, had worked tirelessly for St Peter's over more than four decades. S. Harvie Clark was the vicar, B.C. Lawrence and T.M. Lee the churchwardens, and the architect was K.J. Grice. The stone was laid on 22 June

147 *A coronation party at St Peter's in 1953.*

148 *A version of BBC Town Forum visits Harborne in 1955.*

1963, and the appearance of the church front greatly changed by the new arrangements. The old vicarage had been an interesting landmark, but seemed a white elephant in the post-war years. The church was joined to the new hall by a cloister, providing a dry route after services and used as a place to site memorials to the dead.

Other churches were also rebuilt. Harborne Baptist church was demolished in 1971 and a new church built on a site in Harborne Park Road, taking in the old mission room of St Paul's as a church hall. The Salvation Army's move from the High Street site to its wooden building in Lonsdale Road came in the late 1990s. St Mary's retained most of the old church in its expansion programme; the original Harborne Lodge buildings are used as meeting rooms and accommodation. The site of several large Victorian houses at the south end of Lordswood Road (including the one-time residence of W.H. Auden) was purchased by Seventh Day Adventists, who built a new brick church centre behind an attractive lawn. St John's church was rebuilt on the site of the old St John's School and memorial hall, between the library and the then police station. The church has developed as one of the major evangelical C. of E. churches in Birmingham. The site of the Baptist church was used for a most unsuitable development, 'Techno House', which paved the way for this part of the village to become a wind tunnel between high buildings, quite out of scale with the original two-storey houses, Harborne Terrace and Poyner's Farm. These mistakes are now to some extent being mitigated by a more sensitive redevelopment of Techno House.

With the rise of television, the two Harborne cinemas faced falling attendances and on 13 April 1957 the 'Old Harborne' closed. For some time it lay empty before being sold to the Harborne Village Social Club in whose hands it remains. The Royalty, a much grander cinema, had been the property of Selly Oak Pictures Ltd, but was taken over by Associated British Cinemas. It was eventually closed on 2 November 1963 to become the Mecca Bingo Hall. In this role it has remained a popular attraction for Harborne and beyond. Neighbouring cinemas at Beech Lanes (the 'Warley Odeon') and Selly Oak (the 'Oak') closed and the sites were used for office building or road widening.

149 *A procession for the summer fair in Old Church Road.*

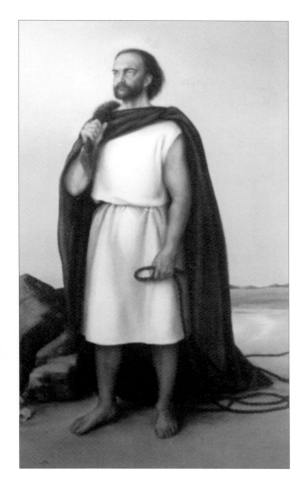

150 *On 24 June 1973 Dawn Cookson presented her new painting of St Peter (shown left) to the parish church. The painting now hangs near the organ.*

151 *The BBC's Dan Archer (shown above) opens the summer fair. The Archers was probably conceived in Harborne, when Edward J. Mason lived in Wentworth Road.*

A useful addition to arts facilities in Harborne came when Birmingham Education Committee decided to use Tennal School (originally the Industrial School, in Balden Road) as the Martineau Teachers' (later 'Education') Centre, moving from Bristol Road, Edgbaston. This has provided new premises for the Harborne Orchestra, founded in the 1940s in the Clocktower. The orchestra is financed as part of the Adult Education Programme. It gives concerts in and around Harborne and rehearses regularly on Friday evenings. The Clocktower itself, formerly High Street School, makes another very pleasant community meet-ing place. In the classrooms (remembered by many old Harbornites) the Harborne Society holds its Art Exhibitions, and they have been the venue for political meetings, forums and adult classes of all sorts. The clock itself, made by William Gardner in the 19th century, is currently working well and giving shoppers the correct Harborne time (which is supposed to be the same as Greenwich). William Gardner's shop was nearly opposite the lower end of Station Road, and originally had a clock set in the wall which advertised his business.

During the war Harborne Railway had been kept open to deliver coal. By 1950 the

152   *A tree in the churchyard, blown down in the storm of January 1954.*

153   *Miss Wheeler was for many years the cub mistress at St Paul's room.*

line had become a curiosity, and on 3 June the Stephenson Locomotive Society ran a special passenger train up to Harborne, and a number of similar special trains were run over the following years. However, as central heating took over from coal the railway's days were numbered. In 1953 ten wagons and a brake van broke away from a train near the main line at Monument Road and ran down the line, falling off and ending in the canal. The junction with the Harborne line caused delay on the main line, and it was decided to close. The last goods train ran in 1963, and there was a final special passenger train, crowded with 300 people, on 2 November of that year. The trackbed was cleared and a walkway laid in 1981-2. It was proposed to demolish the bridge over Park Hill Road. The Harborne Society campaigned for the bridge to be retained and this battle was finally won, with the bridge remaining open for pedestrians.

In February 1988 there was considerable shock in Harborne and beyond when it was proposed to close the municipal golf course (Church Farm, the land which included County Field, Warstones and was bordered by the old Steampot Lane) and build houses. Harborne had all too few open spaces and recreational facilities. An open meeting was held and an action committee formed. There had been no public consultation, and it appeared that the council had moved on insufficient knowledge of the facts. Fifteen hundred leaflets were produced by the action committee before a public meeting, called by the council at short notice. As a compromise the committee proposed that the course should be kept open for a trial period of 12 months. This was finally agreed; the trial of course proved the value of the

154 *Advertisements from a* Birmingham Post *shopping supplement of 1965.*

golf course, not only to those in Harborne, but for miles around, and the golf course was saved.

Charles Parker's *Radio Ballads* and Edward J. Mason's *The Archers* were not the only media productions to have been conceived or executed in Harborne. BBC TV has used local scenes to screen *The Doctors*, and at one time a shop in Park Hill Road became 'Acorn Antiques' in a series starring Victoria Wood and Smethwick-born Julie Walters. Harborne was also a setting for the detective stories of Judith Cutler, who has lived in Woodville Road.

Harborne and Quinton Community Festival

SATURDAY, JULY 3rd

TO

SATURDAY, JULY 10th 1976

Lucky Prize Programme   Price 10p

155 *A programme for the Harborne Festival held on Saturday 10 July 1976. Now renamed 'Carnival', the festival is still held annually.*

At the end of the 20th century there was a shift away from traditional names for public houses. Locally, one of the first manifestations of this was in Smethwick, where it was proposed to change the name of the *Blue Gates*, which commemorates the toll gate nearly opposite. This actually happened, although the name was quickly restored after an outcry, but in Harborne several historic pubs have lost their real names, despite the fact that as landmarks they were receiving much publicity for the traditional names. The most unfortunate case is the *King's Head*, a very historic name. However, this has been partly remedied by the new sign erected by the council naming the road junction 'King's Head Cross'. The *Golden Cross* was renamed but has reverted to its original name at the suggestion of the Harborne Society. There was controversy about the *Green Man*, but it eventually retained its name, while the *Court Oak* was refurbished with its original external decoration. There has never been any change at the *Bell*, while the *White Swan*, at the foot of Chad Hill in Edgbaston, but near the furthest extent of Harborne Heath, has survived an attempt to call it the 'Dirty Duck'. The *Junction* currently runs under another name. The landmark *Duke of York* was actually demolished in 2003, the first pub to vanish entirely. The housing to replace it is called 'Lords', possibly in order to echo the name of Lordswood Road.

A contrary trend has been the setting up of conservation areas by Birmingham City Council. These are (a) the area round the church, including Harborne House, the *Bell*, the church and Harborne Hall (many of the buildings within this area are listed); (b) Moor Pool estate, including Carless Avenue, parts of Ravenhurst Road, and the Moor Pool; (c) Greenfield Road, including some long gardens and Victorian houses. The insistent problem of traffic in Harborne has been helped by introducing a one-way system. In the last years of the 20th century there were further efforts to solve the traffic problems in Harborne by introducing more one-way streets and running bus services 448 and 636 to connect with University station, where there is increased frequency on the cross-city line, currently to ten minutes. To begin the 21st century a number of very successful conversions of old buildings have been made. The fire station, relinquished by West Midlands Fire Service after a new station was completed at California, was turned into flats. The same process has been most successfully carried out at the Institute, preserving the building opened by Henry Irving. On the other hand, total demolition was the fate of the old mews (Harrison's and previously Poyner's Farm) and the bus garage, and the area round the old *Duke of York* has changed greatly. Many new homes have been built on these sites, thus adding to the currently intractable traffic problem. Various solutions have been proposed and a one-way system has been introduced in recent years. St Mary's Road has speed bumps to discourage use, but it has seemed impractical to ban parking on the High Street. Harborne Society proposals for low but multi-storey car-parks have not been able to be fulfilled. It has been suggested that the Harborne Railway should be used for a rapid transit system. A current plan for a modern tram along the Hagley Road, with a branch to Bartley Green, which would

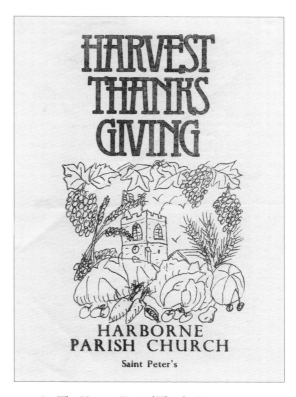

156 *The Harvest Festival Thanksgiving programme in St Peter's on 23 September 1984.*

have the effect of allowing Harborne to be by-passed, is stalled for lack of finance.

Pressure on space is not easily cured, and it is hard to discern Harborne's future. Landowners and developers naturally want to maximise their assets, but conversions of old or historic buildings (including many examples in Birmingham city centre) show that buyers or tenants may be more attracted to a well modernised period house or flat with character than to a poorly designed modern building. It is to be hoped that a large number of 'gentlemen's' residences from Victorian times in Harborne will continue to exist in revived forms.

Bibliography

Printed sources

Clarke, R., *Old Harborne* (Alan Sutton, 1994)

Guest, A.C. and D., *Harborne and Smethwick Tithe Apportionment, 1839-1843* (Eusebia Books, 1988)

Hackwood, F.W., *Some Records of Smethwick* (Smethwick Telephone, 1896)

Hampson, M., *Harborne, The Second Series* (Tempus, 2002)

Hardwick, W.E., *Harborne: A series of Articles from Harborne Parish Church Magazine, 1935-1941* (Birmingham Reference Library 470153)

Jephcott, W.E., *Smethwick and Round About: Cuttings from the Smethwick Telephone, 1951-57* (Smethwick Library)

Kenward, J.H., *Harborne and its Surroundings*, 2nd edition (Cornish, 1885)

'Presterne, Tom' [Thomas Priest], *Harborne Once Upon a Time* (Cornish, 1913)

Stephens, W.B., *A History of the County of Warwick, Vol. VII, The City of Birmingham (Victoria History of the Counties of England)* (OUP, 1964)

Wilmot, F., *The History of Harborne Hall* (Meridian, 1991)

Wright, D., *An Account of Harborne* (Birmingham Public Libraries, 1981)

Manuscript sources

The chief collections of manuscript sources for Harborne history are at:

City of Birmingham Archives

Harborne Branch Library (Donald Wright Collection)

Lichfield Record Office

The National Archives, Kew

St Peter's Church, Harborne (now mainly transferred to the Diocesan Records, City of Birmingham Archives)

Staffordshire Record Office and William Salt Library, Stafford

Index

Numbers in **bold** refer to illustration page numbers.